W9-DFV-219

The Thirteen Colonies

Delaware

Books in the Thirteen Colonies series include:

The Thirteen Colonies

Delaware

Stuart A. Kallen

Lucent Books, Inc.
10911 Technology Place, San Diego, California 92127

975.1
KAL

Cover Photo: Landing of Devries colony at Swaanendael, Lewews, Delawar, 1631 by Stanley M. Arthurs

Library of Congress Cataloging-in-Publication Data

Kallen, Stuart A., 1955–
    Delaware / by Stuart A. Kallen.
        ISBN 1-56006-989-9 (hbk. : alk. paper)
        1. Delaware—History Colonial period, ca. 1600–1775—Juvenile literature. 2. Delaware—History—Revolution, 1775–1783—Juvenile literature. [1. Delaware—History—Colonial period, ca. 1600–1775. 2. Delaware—History—Revolution, 1775–1783.] I. Title. II. Thirteen colonies (Lucent Books)
F167 .K13 2002
975. 1 '02—dc21

2001004070

Copyright 2002 by Lucent Books, Inc.
10911 Technology Place, San Diego, California 92127

No part of this book may be reproduced or used in any other form or by any other means, electrical, mechanical, or otherwise, including, but not limited to photocopy, recording, or any information storage and retrieval system, without prior written permission from the publisher.

Printed in the U.S.A.

2/ 95

Contents

Foreword

The story of the thirteen English colonies that became the United States of America is one of startling diversity, conflict, and cultural evolution. Today, it is easy to assume that the colonists were of one mind when fighting for independence from England and afterwards when the national government was created. However, the American colonies had to overcome a vast reservoir of distrust rooted in the broad geographical, economic, and social differences that separated them. Even the size of the colonies contributed to the conflict; the smaller states feared domination by the larger ones.

These sectional differences stemmed from the colonies' earliest days. The northern colonies were more populous and their economies were more diverse, being based on both agriculture and manufacturing. The southern colonies, however, were dependent on agriculture—in most cases, the export of only one or two staple crops. These economic differences led to disagreements over things such as the trade embargo the Continental Congress imposed against England during the war. The southern colonies wanted their staple crops to be exempt from the embargo because their economies would have collapsed if they could not trade with England, which in some cases was the sole importer. A compromise was eventually made and the southern colonies were allowed to keep trading some exports.

In addition to clashing over economic issues, often the colonies did not see eye to eye on basic political philosophy. For example, Connecticut leaders held that education was the route to greater political liberty, believing that knowledgeable citizens would not allow themselves to be stripped of basic freedoms and rights. South Carolinians, on the other hand, thought that the protection of personal property and economic independence was the basic foundation of freedom. In light of such profound differences it is amazing that the colonies were able to unite in the fight for independence and then later under a strong national government.

Why, then, did the colonies unite? When the Revolutionary War began the colonies set aside their differences and banded together because they shared a common goal—gaining political freedom from what they considered a tyrannical monarchy—that could be more easily attained if they cooperated with each other. However, after the war ended, the states abandoned unity and once again pursued sectional interests, functioning as little nations in a weak confederacy. The congress of this confederacy, which was bound by the Articles of Confederation, had virtually no authority over the individual states. Much bickering ensued—the individual states refused to pay their war debts to the national government, the nation was sinking further into an economic depression, and there was nothing the national government could do. Political leaders realized that the nation was in jeopardy of falling apart. They were also aware that European nations such as England, France, and Spain were all watching the new country, ready to conquer it at the first opportunity. Thus the states came together at the Constitutional Convention in order to create a system of government that would be both strong enough to protect them from invasion and yet nonthreatening to state interests and individual liberties.

The Thirteen Colonies series affords the reader a thorough understanding of how the development of the individual colonies helped create the United States. The series examines the early history of each colony's geographical region, the founding and first years of each colony, daily life in the colonies, and each colony's role in the American Revolution. Emphasis is given to the political, economic, and social uniqueness of each colony. Both primary and secondary quotes enliven the text, and sidebars highlight personalities, legends, and personal stories. Each volume ends with a chapter on how the colony dealt with changes after the war and its role in developing the U.S. Constitution and the new nation. Together, the books in this series convey a remarkable story—how thirteen fiercely independent colonies came together in an unprecedented political experiment that not only succeeded, but endures to this day.

Introduction

Independence and Prosperity

Delaware is the second smallest state in the United States, composed of three counties that together are larger only than Rhode Island. But Delaware boasts a long, colorful history as old as America itself. The original home of the Lenape Indians, the strategically located peninsula on the East Coast was controlled by Dutch, Swedish, English, and American governments within the first 160 years of its existence.

Before the American Revolution, the small colony of Delaware had to fight to maintain its sovereignty, even from other nearby colonies. At various times it was claimed by New York and Maryland, and was actually part of Pennsylvania for several decades.

However, the strong-willed people of Delaware resisted rule by Pennsylvania and were able to maintain their autonomy, fighting off dominance from the large, powerful neighboring state. In this and other situations, Delaware's small size worked to its advantage—those who lived within the colony's three counties were always close to the capital city whether it was New Castle until 1777 or Dover after that time. With quick access to government offices, Delaware's voters were always able to unite when threatened by outside forces while maintaining close relations with politicians who made decisions for them.

A Central Location

Delaware's location between the southern states of Maryland and Virginia, and the northern states of Pennsylvania and New Jersey has placed it at a crossroads of American history and culture. This

The Thirteen Colonies

Part of Massachusetts

New Hampshire

Massachusetts

L. Ontario

New York

Rhode Island

L. Erie

Connecticut

Pennsylvania

New Jersey

Delaware

Maryland

Virginia

ATLANTIC OCEAN

North Carolina

South Carolina

North America

Colonies

Georgia

centralized location, neither northern nor southern, has allowed Delawareans to forge their own identity while helping its people maintain a high level of prosperity out of proportion to the small size of their state.

Although not nearly as densely populated as the surrounding states, Delaware lies midway between New York City and Washington D.C., between Baltimore and Philadelphia. As these booming population centers grew throughout the seventeenth and eighteenth centuries, the high-quality grains, fruits, vegetables, and other food grown by Delaware farmers was in great demand up and down the Eastern seaboard.

With the Delaware Bay and Atlantic Ocean on their state's eastern border, the people of Delaware flourished by milling and shipping the farmers' bounty to markets in London, Paris, Amsterdam, and elsewhere. By the beginning of the nineteenth century, the grain, cloth, paper, steel, and gunpowder mills of Wilmington, powered by the falling water of the Brandywine River, were some of the busiest manufacturers in the nation. These businesses, in turn, attracted a world-class system of banks and financial institutions that rivaled those of any city on the East Coast.

Diverse Population

The fertile fields and bountiful forests of Delaware lured people to the colony from its earliest days. After the Lenape left the state in the mid-1600s, Dutch, Swedes, Finns, and Germans came from northern Europe, while the English, Welsh, and Scots came from the British Isles.

African slaves were also brought to the state to toil under harsh conditions in fields and cities. Some blacks were able to obtain their freedom; they built their own businesses, schools, and churches, even in the face of eighteenth-century discrimination. But while other southern states kept the institution of slavery alive during the nineteenth century, the people of Delaware had little use for it, and it more or less died out in the state by the early 1800s.

Economic factors contributed to the decline of slavery—Delaware's small farms and booming factories simply did not need to rely on forced labor. But there was also strong support for the ideals written in the Bill of Rights and the U.S. Constitution. And the people of Delaware had always shown an independent streak. Delawareans fought in nearly every battle during the American Revolution, were influential in the Continental Congress, and held positions of key importance while the Constitution was being drafted. They were the first to write a state constitution after independence, and the first to ratify the U.S. Constitution.

As a small state, the people of Delaware raised a loud voice in support of independence. They fought side by side with people from large colonies, and opposed them when they threatened to overshadow their state's sovereign rights. In war and in peace, the Delaware colony set a shining example, and rightly earned the nickname the Diamond State.

Chapter One

First Contact

Delaware is a small state made up of three counties located on the large peninsula that it shares with Maryland. The entire eastern edge of the state lies on the Atlantic Ocean, Delaware Bay, and the Delaware River. Although forty-ninth in size of the fifty United States, the people of Delaware call their home the "First State" because Delaware was first to approve the U.S. Constitution in 1787. Delawareans also call it the "Diamond State" because Founding Father Thomas Jefferson said Delaware was "a jewel among the States,"[1] referring to its small size, rich farmland, and valuable harbors.

The first known inhabitants of Delaware were about twenty thousand members of the Lenape tribe, Native Americans who hunted and farmed across a broad section of present-day eastern Pennsylvania, New Jersey, Delaware, the Hudson River Valley, and the area around New York City. The tribe is sometimes called Lenni-Lenape, and in their native Algonquian language, the term means "common people," or more grandly "We, the People." The tribe was divided into three main bands: the Munsee, or "Wolves," the Unamai, or "Turtles," and the Unalaztako, or "Turkeys."

The Lenape were related to several other bands of Algonquian-speaking tribes including the Powhatan of Virginia, the Mohegans of Connecticut, the Shawnee of Ohio, and the Montauk of Long

Island. The Lenape considered themselves to be the original tribe, or "grandfathers," of all Algonquian-speaking peoples. This belief was widely supported by other tribes in the Northeast who gave the Lenape authority to settle disputes between warring bands.

While the Lenape may have considered themselves the grandfathers of the Algonquian-speaking tribes, they often clashed with their bitter enemies in the region. Warriors from the powerful Five Nations of the Iroquois, who lived in central New York, often paddled their canoes down the Susquehanna River to fight with the Lenape over furs and territory. In addition, the Minqua, a smaller tribe related to the Iroquois, with several thousand members who lived along the Susquehanna River, also fought the Lenape, burning their villages and crops.

Through war and peace, the Lenape inhabited the Delaware region for thousands of years. Their lifestyle was described by Lenape historian Hitakonanu'laxk, or Tree Beard, in *The Grandfathers Speak: Native American Folk Tales of the Lenapé People*:

> For many thousands of years . . . our people and their Algonquin grandchildren lived close to the land. We lived in harmony, and did not despoil the Earth or the living things around us. Our world was pristine, of unparalleled beauty and purity. What we had need of the land gave us. We took only the plant and animal life that we needed and left some for others and for the future generations, or to go to seed and to reproduce. . . .
>
> For food we hunted animals and birds and caught fish. Bear, moose, elk, deer, beaver, etc. were among those animals hunted, as were grouse, turkeys, geese and duck. Fish were caught using lines and bone hooks, speared or caught in weirs and nets. Ocean-run shad were a great food staple along the rivers going to the ocean, as were oysters, clams, etc. among those of our people living on the coast. . . . When an animal was killed, it was thought that the animal gave itself to us, and we gave thanks to it, and offered tobacco to its spirit. Everything that could be used from an animal was

The first known inhabitants of Delaware were the Lenape, who caught fish and hunted moose.

put to use, nothing was wasted. The skins were made into bedding and clothing, the meat was eaten or dried for later use, the bones were made into tools, needles or ornaments, etc. . . . For hunting, we used spears, bolas, and bows and arrows. Our knives were made of flint, as were the points of our arrows and spears.[2]

Lenape women grew corn, beans, pumpkins, squash, and tobacco in fields up to two hundred acres in size. Women also foraged for wild food such as fruit, nuts, and roots. Several varieties of corn were grown including white corn, which was used to make a sort of porridge known as hominy, and blue corn, which was eaten as a finely ground meal. These foods were also mixed with beans, squash, wild herbs, and spices to make stew.

The Lenape lived in large rectangular buildings known as *wikwama* that were built in several different styles. These shelters could be round or oblong and up to sixty feet long and twenty feet wide. The Lenape built them large enough to hold entire extended families including dozens of children, along with parents, aunts, uncles, and grandparents. The *wikwama* had arched roofs or domed roofs and were framed from bent saplings. They were covered with large strips of elm, chestnut, or basswood bark. Inside, food was cooked in fire pits while the smoke escaped through a hole in the roof.

The First Tall Ships

The Lenape lived their lives as they always had until the early seventeenth century, when wooden ships with tall sails appeared off the Atlantic coast. These ships were guided by Europeans who, unlike the Native Americans, had long furry beards. The appearance of these strangers shocked the natives. As trader Adrian Van Der Donck wrote:

> [The] Indians or natives of the land . . . with whom I have conversed, declared freely, that before the arrival of the [first Europeans], they (the natives) did not know that there were any other people in the world than those who were like themselves, much less any people who differed so much [in] appearance from them as we did.[3]

The Lenape lived in *wikwama*, round or oblong structures that could house dozens of family members.

Europeans had been aware of the American continent since at least 1497, when an Italian-born navigator named Giovanni Caboto sailed along the Atlantic coast, probably landing in Canada. Caboto,

The Importance of Tobacco

Tobacco played an important role in the lives of the Lenape and Native American tribes. Lenape author Hitakonanu'laxk, or Tree Beard, talks about tobacco in The Grandfathers Speak: Native American Folk Tales of the Lenapé People:

Tobacco was held to be sacred to us and was not abused. Nor was it a vice to our people as it is in modern culture. First, tobacco, or *ksha'te*, was not inhaled to any great extent.... Also, our Native tobacco is a different kind from that used in modern tobacco products. Tobacco as found today ... [originally came] from ... the Caribbean. Our Native tobacco ... is much stronger and more potent than [modern tobacco]. Usually we mixed herbs and barks with tobacco.... Common mixing ingredients used were: bearberry leaves, red osier dogwood bark, spruce needles, sumach leaves, etc. Tobacco, being sacred, was used to offer smoke in prayer, sending our thoughts to the Creator and spirits. Tobacco was seen as conducive to thinking, and was often smoked when contemplating a problem or situation. It also attracted the spirits to what one was doing and thus it was hoped they would give their blessings to whatever was being undertaken. When a visitor came, they were first offered tobacco and a pipe. Any time people came together in Council, the men would first smoke their pipes, the smoke joining together into one smoke, and their minds into one mind. Any time we killed an animal, picked herbs or plants, planted or harvested crops, before we ate, gave thanksgiving, gave prayer, crossed a stream or started a trip by canoe, tobacco was burned or offered. Our way of life was based on regular thanksgiving for what we received, and tobacco was the medium for this, our offering to the spirits for their blessings and aid.

who worked for the English and changed his name to John Cabot, probably did not sail anywhere near Delaware. After traveling to North America, however, he claimed the entire continent for England in spite of the fact that hundreds of thousands of Native Americans resided there.

In the decades after Cabot's discovery, other Europeans explored the area. In 1524 Italian navigator Giovanni da Verrazano sailed into New York harbor and traded with Native Americans, probably Lenape, near Staten Island. After a cordial meeting, Verrazano attempted to kidnap several women and children, but failed in his efforts.

Verrazano's actions began a long history of tension between the Lenape and white explorers. For the next eight decades, European sailors occasionally arrived on the East Coast only to raid Native American villages for slaves. These sailors, however, left little record of their missions.

Henry Hudson and the Dutch

The next known contact between the Lenape and the Europeans came in 1609, when Henry Hudson, an Englishman working for the Netherlands-based Dutch East India Company, sailed his ship *Half Moon* into Delaware Bay. Hudson was looking for the mythical Northwest Passage, a water route that would allow traders to sail from the East Coast of North America to the Pacific Ocean and on to China. No such route exists but explorers searched for the Northwest Passage from the late fifteenth century until the early nineteenth century.

After searching for the Northwest Passage along the East Coast for several months, Hudson sailed into Delaware Bay on August 28, 1609.

Hudson and his crew traveled up the present-day Delaware River but found the waterway difficult to navigate. Although the *Half Moon* hit several shoals and became stuck in the sand in several places, Hudson's secretary, Robert Juet, had pleasant words for Delaware, described it as "one of the finest, best and pleasantist rivers in the world."[4] However joyful this observation, the men on the *Half Moon* only spent seven hours on the

Delaware, and soon turned around to explore what would later be named the Hudson River.

Hudson returned to Europe in October, disappointing his employers at the Dutch East India Company because he had not found the Northwest Passage. The traders were very happy, however, with the high-quality furs that the explorer had obtained in New York. The Dutch claimed Delaware, New York, New Jersey, and Connecticut for the Netherlands, and planned to send more traders to the area to reap the rich rewards of the land they now called New Netherlands.

Henry Hudson made contact with the Lenape when he sailed the *Half Moon* into Delaware Bay in 1609.

The crew of the *Half Moon*, without Hudson, were put on another ship and sent back to North America with orders to obtain furs from the Native Americans in the New York area. The traders established the first Dutch trading post in America by building some small huts on present-day Manhattan.

An Englishman Names Delaware

The Dutch claim on Delaware did not stop other Europeans from exploring the region. In August 1610, Sir Samuel Argall, the vice governor of a struggling English colony in Jamestown, Virginia, was sailing south from present-day Cape Cod, Massachusetts, with a load of fish to feed the starving Virginians. When a fierce storm blew up, Argall was forced to take refuge in Delaware Bay.

Argall named the cape at the entrance to the bay after the governor of Virginia, Sir Thomas West, third Baron De La Warr. After Argall returned to Virginia, the English began calling the cape, the river, and the bay "Delawarr" or Delaware. The Lenape also became known to the English as the Delaware because of Argall's chance encounter with the region. The name, however, did not take hold right away and the river continued to be called Zueydt or South River by the Dutch, and Poutaxat or Makiriskitton by the Native Americans. (Ironically, Baron De La Warr himself never visited the area that bears his name.)

Dutch Traders and Navigators

Threatened by the English exploration of the area, the Dutch decided to promote a high-profile presence in the New World. The government of the Netherlands promised exclusive trading rights to the first company that charted an accurate map of the region, and this offer inspired several intrepid navigators to explore the area.

In 1614, Cornelius Jacobsen May of Hoorn, Netherlands, sailed up the South River and gave his name to Cape May on the New Jersey side of the river. In 1615, one of May's crewmen, Cornelius Hendricksen, sailed a small ship up the South River to present-day Wilmington. Hendricksen was astonished by what he found when he stopped to trade with some Native Americans who were gathered by the river. According to Harry Emerson Wildes in *The Delaware:*

[Hendricksen] underwent a most surprising shock, for he was greeted in good Dutch by friends whom he had thought long dead. Three Hollanders who had gone north along the Hudson, months ago, were captives living with the Minquas. . . .

The men were ransomed and set free, and from their stories Henricksen compiled reports of the resources of the region that did more to further Dutch enthusiasm for establishing a colony along the Delaware. . . . The explorations of the men gave, moreover, to the Netherlands a clear-cut claim by virtue of discovery of the entire valley of the Delaware [River].[5]

Hendricksen asked the Dutch legislature, called the States General, to grant him exclusive trading rights in the area but was turned down because the States General had signed a treaty with Spain in 1609 in which the Netherlands promised not to sanction official trade in the New World for twelve years.

When the treaty expired in 1621, the States General gave exclusive trading rights in Africa, Asia, and the Americas to the Dutch West India Company. This private corporation was given permission to colonize New York, Delaware, and other East Coast areas. The company had such broad power that it was able to run the new colony like a private kingdom, with its own justice system and even the ability to wage war. And to advance its interests in the New World, the government of the Netherlands gave the Dutch West India Company sixteen warships and a large sum of money.

In 1624, the Dutch West India Company built its first trading post in New Netherlands, called Fort Nassau near present-day Albany. In 1625, the company built a settlement on the site of present-day New York City and called it New Amsterdam. Cornelius May was appointed governor of the new Dutch colony.

May had read Hendricksen's earlier reports on the riches to be found in the Delaware region. Hoping to set up a lucrative trading post in Delaware, May ordered thirty French-speaking Belgians, called Walloons, who were living in New Amsterdam, to settle along the South River near present-day Lewes.

The Dutch rulers, however, had little interest in the area—the river was dangerous and barely navigable, with swift shifting currents and thousands of treacherous sandy shoals. And the fur trade in the area was not as profitable as it was along the Hudson.

The hapless Walloons were left on their own to clear land, build shelters, hunt, fish, establish trading contacts with the Lenape, and survive in a perilous and unfamiliar wilderness. At first soldiers were sent to protect the Belgians, but these men were soon ordered by the governor to move ninety miles upstream to build a fort on the east bank of the Delaware across from present-day Philadelphia. Before the soldiers left, the settlers managed to build one brick house before begging the governor to let them return to New Amsterdam. After little more than a year, the first Dutch settlement in Delaware was abandoned.

The Dutch had little interest in settling Delaware because the Delaware River was treacherous and the fur trade was not very profitable.

Dutch Land Grants

While the Delaware settlement was a failure, New Amsterdam continued to attract settlers, and by the late 1620s more than two hundred people were living there. The Dutch claim on the New World, however, was insecure. French and English sailors continued to fish, trap, and trade along the South River. In order to strengthen their claim on the area, the States General approved a charter for the Dutch West India Company in 1629 called "Freedoms and Exemptions." This charter gave settlers the powers of wealthy European landowners. In *Colonial Delaware—A History,* professor and historian James A. Munroe explains the law:

> The charter encouraged independent settlers by promising them a gift of as much land as they could cultivate properly. But a special incentive was reserved for stockholders in the West India Company. Any stockholder who would settle fifty adults in America might arrange privately to buy from the Indians a tract sixteen miles long on one shore of a river or eight miles long on both shores, running inland as far as was practical. In this tract of land (it could be larger if the settlers numbered more than fifty) the controlling stockholder had the powers, roughly, of a manor lord, and he was given the hereditary title of patroon, equivalent in meaning to the English "patron" but grander in concept. His colonists were to be tax free for ten years but could not leave the land except with the patroon's written consent. The patroon could fish and trade all along the coast between Florida and Newfoundland, but all imports and exports must pass through New Amsterdam and the fur trade remained a monopoly of the company wherever the company had an agent.[6]

Few independent settlers had the financial means to utilize the benefits offered in the Freedoms and Exemptions charter. Even with the promise of free land, a large group of settlers would be required to clear the forest, pull up the tree stumps, and plant enough food crops to insure survival. For wealthy businessmen in the Netherlands, however, the charter offered a way to exploit the riches found in the New World.

The first man to take advantage of the charter was Samuel Godyn, president of the Amsterdam office of the Dutch West India Company. Godyn set up what was called a patroonship with a copper and grain trader named Samuel Blommaert and a diamond merchant named Kiliaen van Rens-

In 1630, Peter Minuit registered the first obtainment of land in Delaware from the Lenape.

selaer. The group hired a sailor named Giles Hossitt to purchase a large tract of land in the "south corner of the Bay of the South River."[7]

Hossitt did his job well, obtaining all of the land from the present-day Cape Henlopen on the southern border of Delaware, north to Bombay Hook—thirty-two miles of riverfront land. For this Hossitt gave the Lenape several hundred dollars worth of axes and cloth. After the land was purchased, Hossitt obtained piles of animal furs from the Lenape, and when they were shipped to Amsterdam, the profits on the sales more than paid for the land purchase. The first land acquisition in Delaware was registered by Peter Minuit, governor of New Netherlands, on July 15, 1630.

Tragedy in the Valley of the Swans

Godyn and his partnership had only four years to settle the land under the provisions of the Freedoms and Exemptions charter. The patroons hired a sailor named David Pietersen de Vries who sent a large ship named *Whale*, filled with settlers. According to Munroe, the ship contained twenty-eight men, "a cargo of lime, brick, tiles, horses, cows, ammunition, provisions, merchandise, and equipment not only for farming but also for whaling. Godyn and his associates were eager to get a supply of whale oil from the whales they were told frequented Delaware Bay."[8]

When the settlers landed in the area in the spring of 1631, thousands of migratory birds filled the nearby wetlands, so the Dutchmen named the area Zwannendael, or Valley of the Swans. The new arrivals built a large brick house and surrounded it with a tall, fortresslike fence called a palisade made from sharpened upright sticks. Once the grounds were secure, they began to cut trees and till the land to plant crops.

Giles Hossitt was placed in charge of the colony and as the crops began to grow, the Dutch were optimistic that their new settlement would thrive. Hossitt befriended the local Native Americans, offering them gifts and extra trade goods for their generous land sale. In return, the Lenape sold him another tract of land on the eastern shore of Delaware Bay. Relations were friendly and the Dutch settlers traded beer brewed with corn and persimmons for fish and game caught by the Native Americans.

Unfortunately there was a cultural clash between the settlers and the Native Americans that would become all-too-common in later years. The Dutchmen believed that they had purchased the land and could do whatever they wished with it. The Lenape did not understand the concept of owning land, and thought that the trade goods were given to them so that they might let the settlers temporarily use the land.

In order to make the Dutch position clear, Hossitt hung up a tin sign by the settlement signifying ownership. On it was painted the coat of arms from the High and Mighty Lords, States General of the Free United Netherlands. Hossitt then invited the local Native Americans to partake in a ceremony and feast. A gun salute was fired and a banquet of cheese, fish, pork, pudding, and beer was offered to the Lenape.

After the meal, as the Native Americans were leaving, one of them innocently decided he wanted the tin sign to make pipes, so he pried it from its post and left. Although no one knows what happened next, de Vries pieced together the story when he returned to Zwannendael from a trading mission on December 3, 1632, and talked to some Native Americans.

De Vries wrote that when it was discovered that the sign was missing, Hossitt became irate, interpreting the theft of the esteemed coat of arms as a supreme insult—as if the natives had burned a Dutch flag. When the Dutchman made his displeasure known to the Lenape, the Native Americans killed the thief and brought his head to Hossitt. This further enraged the Dutchman who did not think the crime warranted such harsh treatment.

Several days later, friends of the dead Native American approached the settlement with beaver skins to trade. When the major Dutch trader came to look at the furs, the Native Americans smashed his head with an ax. They then proceeded to the fields where the rest of the Dutchmen were working. The settlers did not know what was happening, and having had friendly relations until that time, had no reason to run away. The Lenape attacked the Dutchmen and killed every one of them. Then they killed all the cattle and held a feast. The Dutch settlement in the Valley of the Swans had ended in disaster.

The Cultivated Land

Although Zwannendael was destroyed, the failed settlement ultimately had a long-lasting effect on Delaware history. By the 1630s, Great Britain had claimed all of the land along the East Coast from North Carolina to Maine, in spite of Dutch land declarations to the contrary. In 1632, when Cecilius Calvert, the second Lord Baltimore, obtained the land grant for the area that would later become Maryland, the document granted Baltimore only lands that were, in the Latin words of the charter, *hactenus*

In 1632, Cecilius Calvert procured a grant for uncultivated land that would later become Maryland.

inculta, or "hitherto uncultivated." Since the Dutch at Zwannendael had planted crops along the west shore of the South, or Delaware River, this area was considered cultivated and was left out of the Maryland charter. As a result, when English settlers arrived in the area, they set up plantations along the Chesapeake Bay in Maryland, and left the dense woods of Delaware to the Dutch.

Although the land that was once the province of the Lenape would remain undeveloped for the next several years, the Europeans would not miss another opportunity to build outposts in Delaware. With rich fertile lands, a mild climate, and an abundance of natural resources, Delaware would soon become an attractive destination for thousands of people from Europe and beyond.

Chapter Two

European Settlement

From 1609, when Henry Hudson first sailed into Delaware Bay, until the 1630s, there was little European progress in settling Delaware. The hapless Dutch colonists trying to farm the area fell victim to untamable wilderness and hostile Native Americans. But the success of the Dutch elsewhere in the New World, especially in New Amsterdam, had garnered the attention of Sweden's King Gustavus Adolphus who, during his reign, had made Sweden one of the most powerful nations in Europe.

By the time the Dutch colony at Zwannendael had failed in 1632, the armies of Gustavus controlled the region around the Baltic Sea and had conquered parts of present-day Germany, Austria, Hungary, and the Czech Republic. And like nearly every other European ruler at the time, Gustavus was anxious to establish a colony in North America to add to his country's prestige, power, and wealth. The king was killed in the Battle of Lutzen in 1632, however, before seeing his dream become reality.

The king's only daughter, six-year-old Christina, became queen of Sweden, leaving the kingdom to be governed by five of Gustavus's highest advisers until the little girl was old enough to rule. The most powerful of these advisers, Axel Oxenstjerna, was

Sweden's King Gustavus Adolphus died before his dream of establishing a North American colony came true.

approached by William Usselinx of the Dutch West India Company who was interested in colonizing North America as a long-term investment. Oxenstjerna agreed to finance the New Sweden Company, a business that would settle a colony on the South, or Delaware River. To advance its goals, the company hired Peter Minuit, the governor of New Netherlands, to serve on its board of directors. By 1637, the company had a charter and was ready to build in the New World.

New Sweden

In December 1637 Minuit set sail from Sweden in a warship, the *Kalmar Nyckel (Key of Kalmar)*, followed by a smaller transport vessel, the *Bird Griffin*. The ships were loaded with colonists, farming tools, provisions, alcohol, guns, and ammunition. They also carried goods such as colored cloth, axes, toys, mirrors, and other inexpensive items to trade with the Lenape. The sixty or seventy prospective colonists aboard the ship were a group of misfits such as poachers, petty thieves, and army deserters that Swedish officials wanted removed from their country. An unknown number of men were political prisoners from Finland, a country that bordered Sweden and whose residents often clashed with the Swedes over religious practices and territory boundaries.

The trip through the icy winter storms of the Atlantic was long and dangerous, and the expedition did not reach Delaware until the end of March 1638. When the Swedish ships did finally sail into Delaware Bay, the shad and sturgeon were making their spring run up the rivers to spawn. The Minqua were taking advantage of this annual rite, and had come down from their lodges up north to camp and fish.

Remembering the tragic fate of the previous white settlers at Zwannendael, Minuit did not want to stop to trade with the Native Americans even though hostilities between the groups had ceased by then. Instead the expedition sailed up to a natural rocky landing where a small creek flowed into the bay. Minuit named the river Christina Creek in honor of the then twelve-year-old queen of Sweden. The colonists disembarked and unloaded their provisions on the shore to start the colony of New Sweden, near an area now known as The Rocks in present-day Wilmington.

On March 29, in order to attract the attention of the Lenape who lived in the area, Minuit fired several shots from the cannons aboard the *Kalmar Nyckel*. When the Native Americans arrived to see what the commotion was about, Minuit invited five sachems, or chiefs, aboard the ship.

The Europeans proceeded to purchase the land by having the sachems sign long, complicated legal documents written in Dutch. The Lenape could not read, and as happened earlier at Zwannendael, the Native American chiefs did not understand that the New Sweden Company expected to control the land forever, as C. A. Weslager describes in *New Sweden on the Delaware: 1638–1655*:

> There was no haggling over a price because the Lenape concept of land tenure was entirely different from European traditions of land ownership and sale. . . . To the Lenape land was like air, sunlight, or the waters of a river— a medium necessary to sustain life. The idea of an individual exclusively owning the soil was as alien to their thinking as owning the air one breathed or the cool water bubbling from a woodland spring. . . . Land "ownership" meant the right to use the land, to plant on it, to hunt the animals that lived on it, and to build wigwams on it, but not to possess it permanently in the sense that it belonged to one person or family in perpetuity.
>
> The five Lenape chiefs were under the impression they were granting Minuit and his people the right to share the land with them. When they affixed their marks to the deeds

they did not know they were transferring permanent ownership to the Swedes. It was not their intent to give up their right to continue to use the land; they meant their action as a genuine gesture of hospitality.[9]

In return for the sachems' hospitality, Minuit took legal possession of approximately sixty-seven miles of shoreline along Delaware Bay, with no western boundary named at all. After the sachems had signed their marks to the deed, the ship's cannons were fired again, and the Swedish queen's coat of arms was planted in the sand. Minuit christened the land New Sweden.

Building New Sweden

The colonists immediately set about building a fort at "The Rocks" from which they could trade tobacco they had imported from Virginia for furs trapped by Delaware's Native Americans. This outpost, named Fort Christina, was surrounded by a palisade fence with cannons at three corners and a Swedish flag at the fourth. The fort was easily defended because it was strategically located with thick forests on one side and tidal marshes on the other three. Visitors could only approach the fort by canoe, rowboat, or on a narrow path cut through the woods.

While the settlers were able to build their fort within four months, it did not take long for the Dutch, who believed they controlled the area, to protest the presence of the Swedish outpost. The governor of New Amsterdam, William Kieft, informed Peter Minuit in a letter that Dutch nationals had been slaughtered at Zwannendael and, "that the whole South river of the new Netherlands . . . hath already, for many years, been our property, occupied by our forts, and sealed with our blood. . . . We do, therefore, protest against all the disorder and injury, and all the evil consequences of bloodshed, uproar, and wrong which our Trading Company may thus suffer."[10]

The Dutch governor's strong words meant little, since the Netherlands and Sweden were European allies, and Dutch soldiers could not attack a fort flying a Swedish flag. For his part, Minuit ignored the letter and loaded the *Kalmar Nyckel* with

Swedish settlers in Delaware built log cabins like this one in the early eighteenth century.

1,770 beaver pelts, 314 otter pelts, and 132 bear pelts he had obtained from the Lenape.

Having successfully started a Swedish colony in Delaware, Minuit set sail for the West Indies where he planned to do some trading before returning to Sweden. One night on the island of St. Christopher, Minuit was visiting aboard the *Flying Deer*, another Dutch ship. A huge storm came up and blew the ship out to sea. The *Flying Deer*, its crew, and Minuit were never seen again. After waiting a short time for Minuit to return, sailors on the *Kalmar Nyckel* assumed he was dead and returned to Stockholm.

While the several thousand furs aboard the *Kalmar Nyckel* were valuable, the stockholders in the New Sweden Company found the tobacco Minuit had obtained in Virginia to be worth even more. It seemed that the European public could not get enough of the addictive substance and prices for tobacco products were high. The stockholders in the New Sweden Company happily discovered that the investment in ships, men, and provisions for New Sweden had nearly paid for itself in less than six months.

Governor "Big Belly" Printz

Recognizing the value of their holdings in the New World, the Swedish government bought out the Dutch investors in the New

Life Inside Fort Christina

The settlers at Fort Christina were mostly woodsmen accustomed to life in the forests of Sweden and Finland. It did not take them very long to construct a comfortable and useful fort at their Delaware outpost. Anna T. Lincoln writes in Wilmington, Delaware: Three Centuries Under Four Flags:

Within [the palisades of the fort] were two houses built of rough logs, one of them was used for a dwelling and the other for a magazine [arsenal] or store-house. The dwelling house had loopholes [through which weapons may be fired] and perhaps two or more windows. The roof was gabled and covered with split timbers. There were two rooms, one was used for both dining room and sleeping quarters. The fireplace and oven were built of bricks brought over in the ship. Chairs, a table, and rough benches made of split timbers completed, with the beds, the rough furniture. The land inside the palisade was tilled and a garden of herbs planted. The enclosure was large enough to give shelter to the whole colony in case of alarm; commodious enough to furnish a market-place for the trade and sale of merchandise; to hold the governor's residence, and the great central store-house in which to store all the goods. Here public worship was held, and later a little chapel was built within the fortifications. Near "The Rocks" and perhaps inside the palisade was a cave, large and clean, over six feet high, enriched by a spring of sparkling water which rose in a corner and flowed over the smooth rock-bottom until it found an outlet. . . . The building of the fort was a laborious undertaking but it was finished before the thirty-first of July in the year that the Swedes landed.

Sweden Company. In 1640, another group of settlers was sent to Fort Christina under the leadership of Peter Hollender Ridder who had been named governor of New Sweden. This group was soon followed by Dutch settlers sailing under the Swedish flag. And in 1641, fifty Swedish soldiers, and a group of Finnish men and women arrived, bringing with them goats, horses, sheep, cattle, and seed for grain.

Under the rule of Governor Ridder, settlers at Fort Christina faced food shortages and a continued threat from the nearby Dutch colony. For added protection, Ridder asked the Swedish government to send more soldiers and colonists, and in January 1643, three Swedish warships sailed up the Delaware Bay. One of them contained Ridder's replacement, John Printz, a cavalry major in the Swedish army. When the Native Americans saw the four-hundred-pound Printz, they named him "Big Belly" and the name stuck.

The large man immediately began an aggressive campaign to improve the lives of the struggling colonists in New Sweden, buying large quantities of food and livestock from citizens in New Amsterdam. Printz also began carrying out detailed instructions from the New Sweden Company containing twenty-eight articles, or directives, that he was to follow in the new colony. These included planting enough corn to make the colony's food supply self-sufficient; growing as much tobacco as possible; experimenting with ways to desalinate seawater so it would be drinkable; searching for gold and minerals; harvesting nuts from wild oak and walnut

John "Big Belly" Printz aggressively improved the lives of colonists in New Sweden by implementing directives of the New Sweden Company.

trees; establishing a whale-hunting business; and even raising silkworms for silk production. The governor was also instructed to oversee the behavior of the settlers, punishing those who "will not live quietly and peacefully,"[11] and instructing people in the articles of the Christian faith.

Meanwhile, Ridder had purchased more parcels of land from the Native Americans for the Swedish colony including vast tracts of acreage on both sides of the South River as far north as present-day Trenton, New Jersey. Printz, the former soldier, took on the task of establishing Swedish dominance on the South River. He constructed an imposing, heavily armed garrison named Fort Elfsborg about three miles upstream from Fort Christina, from which he could control Dutch shipping traffic to Fort Nassau. He evicted English colonists who had settled in the area.

On an island the Native Americans called Tinicum, Printz built the first white settlement in Pennsylvania, Fort New Gothenburg, named for the city in Sweden where the holding company was based. When construction was completed, the governor moved the capital of New Sweden from Fort Christina to the island.

In 1644, Printz also took care of his own lavish tastes, building "Printz Hall," his place of residence, high on a hill above Fort New Gothenburg. With a commanding view of the region, the governor's log mansion was by far the fanciest building in New Sweden with imported glass windows and a library full of expensive books. The closet of the governor's wife held over $2,000 worth of European clothing—a huge sum at that time. Unfortunately, the mansion was accidentally destroyed by fire little more than a year after its construction.

The Dutch Take the Delaware

Printz was an arrogant governor who treated the settlers like slaves and executed those who complained. But for ten years, he built New Sweden up to its greatest strength in the New World. However, Peter Stuyvesant, the new Dutch governor of New Netherlands, was not impressed by Printz.

In 1651, Stuyvesant sent eleven ships up the Delaware to build Fort Casimir downstream from Fort Christina, thereby taking control of the river. There was little Printz could do—the government in Sweden was occupied with other matters and was seriously neglecting the needs of the colony. The frustrated Printz returned to Sweden in 1654 to ask for reinforcements, and in his absence was replaced by Johan Rising who evicted the Dutch from Fort Casimir.

In late August 1655, Stuyvesant sent seven ships and six hundred men into Delaware Bay. By mid-September, the Dutch had retaken their fort, placed seven land-based cannons in positions aimed at Fort Christina, and ordered Rising to surrender. When the Swedish governor failed to respond, the Dutch soldiers proceeded to slaughter the settlers' farm animals, destroy their orchards, and burn their homes. Israel Acrelius describes what happened:

> The flower of the Swedish male population were at once torn away and sent over to New Amsterdam. . . . The men were taken by force and placed on shipboard; the women at home in the house were abused, their property carried off, and their cattle slaughtered.[12]

The Swedes were defeated, the flag of the Netherlands flew over Fort Christina, and the Dutch now had control of the entire South River. The new rulers allowed any member of the defeated colony to stay only if they swore allegiance to the Dutch States General. Those who would not were sent back to Sweden. Peter Stuyvesant, using the largest naval fleet ever deployed in the New World, had ended the seventeen-year colonial experiment called New Sweden.

The Capital at New Amstel

Stuyvesant appointed Jean Paul Jaquet to govern the settlements along the South River and moved the capital of the colony to a little town outside of Fort Casimir. Jaquet set about improving the area, ordering the construction of roads and bridges while selling off marked lots sixty feet wide and three hundred feet deep.

The cost of retaking the colony from the Swedes, however, threatened the Dutch West India Company with bankruptcy. To stave off financial ruin, the shareholders asked the wealthy city of Amsterdam, Netherlands, for financial assistance. Amsterdam's city fathers believed that they might profit from such a partnership, and began sending people and supplies to the capital of the Delaware colony near Fort Casimir that they now called New Amstel.

By 1657 Jaquet had been replaced by Jacob Alrichs, whose title was vice director. Alrichs brought about two hundred colonists, soldiers, and servants to New Amstel and began building up the village with a town hall, a wharf, a bakery, a school, and other structures. Within a year, New Amstel had over one hundred buildings. Although the region had been taken by force from the Swedes, the colony now returned to its sleepy existence. According to Jeanette Eckman:

> After the surrender of Fort Christina in 1655, a few Dutch soldiers were stationed there to keep an eye upon the Swedish planters and their officers. But in this peaceful community the soldiers seemed to have paid more attention to their gardens and other interests than to the fort . . . for the [fort] buildings became dilapidated and complaint was made of it as the haunt of smugglers of tobacco and other commodities.[13]

The change from Swedish to Dutch ownership did little to improve the fortunes of the colony. Several seasons of bad weather destroyed food crops and a fever epidemic killed dozens of settlers, mostly children. As the epidemic raged, another ship full of settlers arrived bringing the population of New Amstel to six hundred. The new arrivals had little to eat, however, and sickness and starvation became a constant threat.

During this time of trouble, soldiers working for Lord Baltimore of Maryland rode into the colony and tried to cause conflict between the local Native Americans and the Dutch. Rumors of an English takeover swept through the colony and many settlers decided that life was better in Maryland. Soon the population of South River colony had fallen to less than thirty families.

With these ongoing problems, the Dutch trading company was having a very difficult time providing funds for the colony's defense and general expenses. The stockholders finally gave up their rights to the colony to the city of Amsterdam under the provisions that more soldiers be sent to defend the colony and a mile of land be cleared and settled every year. Amsterdam did its part, and by 1663, the Dutch colony was once again thriving with over 110 plantations owned by Swedish, Dutch, and Finnish farmers.

The English Take Control

By this time, the English were well established on the East Coast of America. They had powerful and prosperous colonies in Massachusetts, Connecticut, Virginia, Maryland, and elsewhere. These colonies had the financial backing of the powerful king of England, Charles II, and his brother James, the duke of York. Both men had a strong desire to seize the Dutch colonies in the New World and take total control of America.

In August 1664, English warships sailed into present-day New York harbor. The ships were under orders from the duke of York to take New Amsterdam by force. Stuyvesant and the local residents knew they were outgunned and surrendered peacefully on August 27. In honor of the duke, the colony was renamed New York, and New Amsterdam was named New York City.

By the end of September, two small English warships had been dispatched to the Delaware colonies under the command of Robert Carr. After a small skirmish in which three Dutch soldiers were killed, the English seized New Amstel and plundered the town. Dozens of Dutch, Swedish, and Finnish citizens were sold into slavery and their property was confiscated by the English. Those who remained were made subjects of King Charles II.

Carr was put in charge of supervising the Delaware colony, and he told the citizens there that they "shall enjoy their barns, houses, lands, goods, and chattels with the same privileges and on the same terms as they now possess them, only that they change masters."[14]

The English government let Delaware residents know that they would not lose their way of life after the Dutch turned over control of the colonies.

In 1672 New Amstel was renamed New Castle and English weights and measures came into use. English monetary units of the shilling and penny replaced the Dutch florin and stiver. Now that the Delaware was controlled by England, settlers from Maryland, New Jersey, Virginia, and New York, where cleared land was growing scarce, flooded into the small colony.

Although the powers that governed Delaware had changed once again, life remained the same for the average citizen, as Eckman writes:

It was a sparsely settled community of individualists of differing ideas and temperaments. Everyone knew everyone else, each fellow spoke his mind, quarreled and protested when he believed his rights interfered with, accepted the established social order without being [submissive] or much of a respecter of persons, and joined his dearest enemy in defense of the right of the small strip of territory to exist as an indivisible entity. The frequent changes of absentee ownership seemed only to cement this local conception of a special and peculiar privilege and destiny.[15]

Land Grants to William Penn

While the settlers of Delaware struggled to grow crops and survive in the wilderness, the English king controlled their fate, giving away large chunks of land to nobles and businessmen with little regard for the citizens who were already there. One of the beneficiaries of this system was William Penn, who was given the entire colony of Pennsylvania, along with Delaware.

Penn was the godson of the duke of York. His father was a war hero and an admiral in the British navy. William Penn, however,

Charles II (center left) granted the colonies of Pennsylvania and Delaware to William Penn (center right).

was unusual among the British upper classes. He was a member of the Society of Friends, also known as Quakers, a then-controversial Protestant religious sect whose teachings were quite unusual in the seventeenth century.

The Friends believed that all people were equal under the eyes of God and that women were equal to men. They refused to take oaths to the government, fight wars, or even take their hats off in the presence of the king since they believed that all were equal. Because of their beliefs they were persecuted by other religious sects. The Puritans who controlled Massachusetts considered Quakers to be heretics and their teachings to be inspired by the devil. In Massachusetts, Quakers were jailed, tortured, and executed.

Because of his father's position, however, William Penn was a member of the ruling class. In addition, King Charles II owed Admiral Penn, who died in 1670, a large sum of money for his honorable service to the British government. The younger Penn asked for a land grant in the New World instead of the money, and the king agreed, seeing that he could pay off his debt to the family and at the same time rid England of the troublesome Quakers who Penn promised to resettle in America.

Charles II gave Penn an area the king called "Pennsylvania" or "Penn's Woods," the largest tract of land in the New World ever given to a person without noble rank or title.

Penn called Pennsylvania, an area larger than the country of Ireland, his "Holy Experiment" and he planned to use the colony as a refuge not only for Quakers, but also for other persecuted peoples in the New World. Penn drew up a charter for the new colony that granted rights such as freedom of speech, freedom of worship, and trial by jury. These ideas, so much a part of modern American culture, were rarely practiced anywhere in the world at that time.

Penn was still not satisfied, however. The land given to him had no access to the ocean because the Delaware colony lay between Pennsylvania and the Atlantic. In 1682, he petitioned the duke of York to give him Delaware, and the duke obliged. Delaware became part of Pennsylvania and the area became known as the "Three Lower Counties of Delaware." These counties, New Castle, Kent, and

Sussex, were to remain part of Pennsylvania until the Revolutionary War in 1776.

Penn initially allowed Delaware to have equal representation in the governing assembly that met in Philadelphia. In 1701, the Three Lower Counties were allowed to have their own legislature.

Although Delaware was now part of Pennsylvania, life continued much as it had before. Survival was often difficult but the natural resources of the New World provided nearly limitless timber, fish, and other necessities for a growing population. And the land's bounty continued to attract immigrants from Europe as German, English, Dutch, and Swedish settlers brought their hopes and dreams to a new land of unlimited possibilities.

Chapter Three

Daily Life in Colonial Delaware

D uring the 1600s the heavily forested peninsula of Delaware was never populated by more than several thousand people. Life was often difficult and survival was dependant on favorable weather, relations with local Native Americans, and the amount of capital expended by European overseers who lived thousands of miles across the Atlantic Ocean.

The colony was inhabited mostly by young, single men from Finland, Sweden, Germany, and Russia who lived in log cabins reminiscent of those in their homelands. A group of men could construct such a cozy cabin in little more than a day. In the early years the workmen were mostly Finns who cut large cedar trees with axes, trimmed off the branches, sawed them to equal length, and shaved an indentation, called a saddle notch, in the end of each log. The logs were piled up to make four walls and the cracks between them were filled with mud. A Swedish botanist named Peter Kalm described the typical cabins found in New Sweden in *Readings in Delaware History* edited by Carol E. Hoffecker:

The houses which the Swedes erected for themselves, when they first came here, were very poor . . . a little cottage built of round logs with the door so low that it was necessary to bend down when entering. As the colonists had no windows with them small loopholes served the purpose, covered with a sliding board, which could be closed and opened. Clay was plastered into the cracks between the logs on both sides of the walls. The fireplaces were made from granite boulders found on the hills, or, in places where there were no stones, out of mere clay. The bakeoven was also made inside the house.[16]

These crude cabins were often topped with an arched roof covered in grass thatch, bark, or wooden shingles. Windows might be made from paper soaked in animal fat, which allowed light to pass through. Inside the cabin, settlers slept on dirt floors or on beds made from piles of grass or dried leaves. Sometimes a slab of log was hinged onto the wall to make a bedstead. Bedrooms might also be above the roof beams in the loft, warmed by the rising heat of the fireplace. Log planks fitted with round legs served as tables and chairs.

Cabins that stayed warm in the winter and cool in the summer were quickly constructed in Delaware.

While these rough-hewn homes were rudimentary by modern standards, they were warm in winter and cool in summer and were built throughout America whenever pioneers moved into a forested area.

Whatever comforts the settlers lacked in their homes, they made up for in the saunas they built for relaxation. These steam rooms, known as *bastu*, had long been a tradition in Sweden and Finland and the early settlers imported them to America. Built along the riverbanks, the one-room saunas were tightly constructed from logs. A large fireplace in the corner was used to heat rocks until they were red hot. The rocks were then removed from the fire and water was poured over them which filled the sauna with steam. The settlers lay on benches and lightly whipped their bodies with birch branches to cause their blood to circulate faster. After an hour in the *bastu*, the hardiest bathers ran outside to jump in the frigid river or roll in the snow during winter.

Religion and Government

By the late seventeenth century, the Three Lower Counties of Delaware had been ruled by Sweden, the Netherlands, Great Britain, and finally by William Penn, who planned to use the region as a homeland for thousands of Quakers who were facing persecution in Europe. Penn's dream of a "Holy Experiment" in the New World brought an unprecedented level of river traffic to Delaware as more than seven thousand Quaker settlers sailed up the Delaware River between 1682 and 1685. Many were on their way to Philadelphia but some stayed in the small towns along the river that had previously been settled by Swedes, Finns, and Dutch.

The original European citizens of Delaware, however, were unhappy with the Quaker takeover of their colony, and much of this discontent was based on religious differences. As James A. Munroe writes in *History of Delaware:*

Delawareans were generally members of the Church of England [Anglicans] who spurned the Quakers as radical sectarians. . . . The Quakers also were newcomers, whose sudden accession to power rankled old settlers. . . . There

Governor Rising Calls for Workers

In 1657, Johan Rising, governor of New Sweden, wrote an official report in which he analyzed the types of workers the struggling colony needed to survive. It was reprinted in Narratives of Early Pennsylvania, West New Jersey and Delaware, 1630–1707, *edited by Albert Cook Myers. Rising wrote:*

What advantage various trades could bring here into the country is self-evident, especially if one could make all kinds of things from these good trees, which could be sold to advantage. Besides timber-cutters, we need some one who can burn tar and make shoemaker's wax, which is here an expensive article; also a soap-maker, since we have a potash-burner with us [for the making of soap]. Besides this there are other materials of the land, which could be taken up and manufactured, as saltpeter [for gunpowder], for … if we could here establish powder-mills it would bring us great profit. . . . Of blacksmiths (aside from gunsmiths) we have enough for our needs, as well as cordwainers [rope makers] and leatherdressers, tailors, skinners, swordmakers, glass makers, masons, house-carpenters, etc. But we have need of pottery-makers, brick-makers, lime-burners, cabinet makers, wooden-basin makers and wooden-plate turners, shoemakers and tanners. . . . A French hat-maker could do much good here; also a winegrower and a bird-catcher who could capture geese and ducks in nets on the low places in spring and fall, since these birds come here by thousands in the fall and spring. Also, if some Dutch farmers could be brought here and settled on the company's own land it would be very useful, and more such things.

was also, particularly in the older town of New Castle, jealousy of Philadelphia and its surge to wealth and power.[17]

These problems were exacerbated because Delaware only had about twenty-five hundred people while Pennsylvania was home to more than twenty thousand. In spite of this distribution of population, both colonies were equally represented in the legislative assembly.

The political problems diminished when Delaware was granted self-rule in 1704. The new government showed a fierce streak of independence that was unique in the colonies at that time. For instance, when the assembly passed new legislation, the lawmakers did not feel the need to send it to England for approval, as did lawmakers in the other colonies.

The Delawareans also allowed white men who owned fifty acres of land or businesses worth £40 to vote. This prevented women, servants, slaves, and the poor from having a voice in government affairs, but was considered liberal by colonial standards since almost any white man could obtain land by petitioning the government. In fact, if a person was eligible to vote, he was required by law to so do or face a fine of twenty shillings—a considerable sum. And this was at a time when it might take a voter an entire day to walk or ride his horse to the nearest polling place.

There were two political parties, the "court" party of wealthy aristocrats, and the "country" party of average farmers. Each October voters in the Three Lower Counties elected tax assessors, representatives for an executive council that advised the governor, and county coroners to investigate unusual deaths.

Voters also elected a sheriff whose job was to enforce court orders, assemble juries for trials, collect taxes, run the county jail, and enforce laws.

There were few courthouses, and trials were usually held in local taverns by judges who rode a "circuit" from one town to the next. Most trials were civil disagreements over land boundaries and failure to pay debts. Occasionally, criminal trials were held for those accused of offenses such as drunkenness, profanity, or stealing horses.

Growing Towns

While politicians busied themselves with writs, taxes, and laws, the Three Lower Counties of Delaware were flourishing with activity. Between 1705 and 1760 the population of the colony increased more than eleven times from three thousand to thirty-five thousand. Workers continued to clear land, drain marshes, build embankments along streams, and construct roads through the forests. The simple log cabins of the past gave way to handsome wood frame homes or those skillfully constructed from brick or stone.

The town of New Castle, on the Delaware River, was a thriving hub of trade with a climate sure to attract immigrants, as Reverend George Ross wrote in 1727:

New Castle is the chief and best Town and most comodiously situated for Trade and Navigation; it stands upon a pleasant Eminence [hill] and is found of late years to be both healthy and agreable and In Sumer is preferrable to any upon [the] Delaware for its Coole and refreshing Breezes and advantages it owes to its being nearer the Sea by 40 Miles than the so much talked of Philadelphia.[18]

Workers on the shipping docks of New Castle spent their days loading ocean-bound ships with barrels full of fresh water, dried meat, and gunpowder. Ships were also laden with items such as beef, cheese, butter, grains, and tanned leather for export to the West Indies and Europe. The purchase of these items was often arranged at the New Castle weekly market established by William Penn in 1682. Meanwhile carpenters and woodworkers prospered by building and repairing ships along the busy docks.

Residents of New Castle were by no means well-to-do, but managed to earn enough money from trade and farming to survive, as Ross writes:

[The people of New Castle are] generally low [poor] in their Condition but not indigent; having wherewithall to Support themselves but little to spare; The Employ and business . . . of them [that] lived in the Town was retailing of Goods, Rum, Sugar and Molasses together with some European Goods, some enjoyed posts in the Government and others got their Living by their handy Crafts, as Carpenters—Smiths and Shoemakers; those of them that

Ships were constructed to carry exports from Delaware to Europe and the West Indies.

had their Residence in the Country, were occupied in clearing and grubbing of Land, in Raising of Grain, as Wheat, Rye, Indian Corn, Oats and Barley; in improving their Stock such as Horses, Horn Cattle, Sheep and Hoggs, few or none of them had [Estates] to support them, without being obliged to their Trade, Labour and Industry.[19]

Besides New Castle, other Delaware towns grew and prospered because of the ever-increasing river traffic. About sixty families lived in Lewes in 1700, and the town port became an important shipping point for grain and meat. The sawmill in the town was kept busy cutting timber into boards for barrels, homes, and ships. Because of its location at the mouth of Delaware Bay, Lewes was also home to a group of skilled river captains who were hired to pilot ships through the sandbars and hazardous shoals on the Delaware River between the Atlantic Ocean and Philadelphia.

The financial advantages of having miles of coastline facing the Atlantic Ocean and Delaware Bay was offset when marauding pirates and privateers attacked unguarded towns. For example, in 1698, over eighty pirates invaded Lewes, entering homes and carting off money, clothes, jewelry, and other valuables. At other times, pirates used the hidden inlets and unpopulated islands in the bay to hide from authorities.

Since coastal and river towns were vulnerable to pirate attack, William Penn ordered the construction of Dover in the central part of the peninsula in 1683. Dover grew quickly and within two decades the city had a courthouse and prison. In 1777, it became the capital of Delaware and remains so today.

Farming and Milling

While some colonists earned money in towns catering to the shipping trade, the Delaware economy was based on agriculture, and the majority of citizens in the colony were farmers or farm- workers. In fact, the population of the colony grew so quickly because thousands of Europeans moved there to obtain inexpensive farmland.

While most European peasants scratched out a meager existence on a few barely productive acres, Dutch and Swedish trading companies offered the first colonists in Delaware as much free land as they could farm. When Great Britain took over, the duke of York made free land grants, usually of one hundred to two hundred acres, to any white man who applied, providing the land was cleared and farmed within a year.

Some recipients received grants of up to ten thousand acres to build dams along streams in order to harness waterpower for grain mills. By the 1700s, Brandywine River was the center of the flour-milling trade in the three Delaware counties. Grains such as wheat, corn, and barley were brought up the Christina River by farmers in small boats called shallops, and burlap sacks filled with flour were shipped back by the same route.

A particularly flavorful strain of wheat was grown in northern Delaware and nearby Pennsylvania. It was brought to the mills at Brandywine River in wagons, and after processing, it was shipped to the finest bakeries of Europe.

The livelihoods of many Delaware residents revolved around the gristmills that processed grain into flour.

Gristmills were the center of financial and social life in the colonial towns and other businesses were built nearby to take advantage of the situation. In the Brandywine River area, a popular food market was built on land owned by Thomas Willing and visitors referred to the area as Willingtown. As the population grew around the mill, the townspeople asked King George II for an official city charter. In 1739, when the English ruler granted the charter it was addressed to the people of Wilmington. Without the consent of the people who lived there, Willingtown had become Wilmington, possibly named for the king's friend, Spencer Compton, the earl of Wilmington.

Hardworking Families

While settlers were attracted to Delaware with the promise of free land, there was always a labor shortage in America. And in an era before farm machinery, agriculture was a backbreaking enterprise practiced with horse, plow, hoe, and ax. Survival in an era before supermarkets meant that farmers had to plant, cultivate, and harvest crops; preserve meat by salting and smoking it; cut wood to heat homes; hunt; fish; and even fashion furniture and tools by hand.

Women worked equally hard, cooking and cleaning house, caring for children, baking bread several times a week, milking cows, churning butter, making beer and wine, tending to the family vegetable garden, and making soap. Most women also had to spin wool and flax, dye the cloth, and make clothing for the entire family.

With so much work to be done, farmers required large families simply to survive. Children as young as four years old were expected to help their parents. Girls learned household skills at their mothers' sides, while boys helped their fathers work in the fields. Children were also assigned specific tasks such as fetching water and firewood, collecting eggs from chickens, tending to young farm animals, and weeding gardens. From the age of ten, boys might hunt or fish to supplement the food on the family table.

Children always had household chores, as girls worked with their mothers in the home and boys helped their fathers in the field.

The hardworking families of Delaware also took the education of their children very seriously. Ross describes the situation in Sussex County in 1728:

> [There] is no publick school in all the County, the General Custom here being for . . . a Neighbourhood (which lies sometimes 4 or 5 miles distant . . . from another) to hire a Person for a certain Term and Sum to teach their Children to read and Write English. For whose accomodation they meet together at a place agreed upon, cut down a Number of Trees, and build a Log house in a few hours . . . whither they send their children every day during the Term; for it ought to be observed by way of commendation of the American Planters now a days that whatever pains or charges it may cost, they seldom omit to have their children instructed in reading and writing the English Tongue.[20]

By the time boys grew up they were usually skilled enough to start their own farms after first petitioning the government for several hundred acres of land. Girls were ready to marry, have children, and run their own households.

Immigration and Indentured Servants

The success of an agricultural colony relied on a constant influx of cheap labor, and by the 1700s, a steady supply of servants and slaves provided the necessary workforce to make Delaware prosper.

In 1717, the Scotch-Irish began to arrive in Delaware. These people were Presbyterians who left the predominantly Catholic country of Ireland to escape high taxes and religious persecution. Most of the Scotch-Irish were poor and could not afford the cost of a ticket to America. Ship captains took advantage of this situation by offering free passage to the colonies if the traveler signed a contract stating he or she would work as an indentured servant for four to seven years. When the captain sailed into New Castle with his servants, he would sell the contracts to farmers and business owners who assembled on the docks in search of cheap labor.

Most of the indentured servants were young men and women between the ages of fifteen and twenty-five. They were paid no wages but received food, shelter, and clothing for their labors. Some were treated cruelly by their masters; others were educated and taught useful skills.

Some indentured servants were honest, hardworking people hoping to get ahead in the colony. Others were criminals, gamblers, or drunks who wanted to escape the law or outstanding debts. Many of these people simply escaped once they reached their destination.

Slavery in Delaware

There were never enough indentured servants to keep up with the demand for labor in Delaware, so black African slaves were brought to the area to make up for the shortage.

The Dutch West India Company was engaged in the slave trade in the early seventeenth century and imported dozens of African slaves to New Netherlands and New Sweden. When the duke of York took possession of the colonies, he imported slaves through The Royal African Company, in which he was a major stockholder.

By the 1720s, about 500 slaves worked as servants and farmhands in Delaware.

Most of the African men, women, and children kidnapped by slavers were sent to Virginia and Maryland, but by the 1720s, there were around twenty-five hundred slaves in Pennsylvania, with about five hundred in the Three Lower Counties of Delaware. Some families had one or two slaves and several wealthy individuals owned large numbers of slaves. A few slaves worked as domestic servants but most were used as farmhands. Slaves also worked as shoemakers, brick makers, bakers, carpenters, tailors, blacksmiths, leather tanners, and in other trades.

Some blacks in the colony were eventually set free in payment for their years of service. Others were able to buy their freedom, but more than 70 percent of the blacks in Delaware at any given time labored as slaves.

As the number of black slaves increased in Delaware, fear of slave revolts motivated legislatures to pass stringent laws against blacks in order to limit their civil rights. In 1700, laws called "For the Trial of Negroes" were passed that prohibited black people from owning weapons of any kind or assembling in groups of more than six. If a black person committed a crime, he or she was sentenced to a longer jail term than a white person who broke the same law. And by 1740, there were enough free blacks that laws were written to prohibit them from voting, holding office, or testifying against white people in court.

While free black Americans experienced active discrimination in Delaware, they were not punished for speaking out against slavery and prejudice, and in favor of equal rights. They were aided by Quakers whose religion forbade the enslavement of any human being. Methodists also opposed slavery and traveled throughout the Delaware counties to teach religion to slaves.

By the time of the Revolutionary War in 1776 there was a large population of free blacks who raised their voices for justice, independence, and equality. After the Revolution, some free Delaware blacks were able to succeed against the odds, as Carol Hoffecker and Annette Woolard write in "Black Women in Delaware's History":

> Among the growing number of free blacks, most women
> were employed as household servants or washer women

and received low wages. Yet, despite these heavy burdens, a few free black women emerged from poverty to achieve education and success. Betty Jackson, a black woman from Chadds Ford, Pennsylvania, established a tea room on French Street in Wilmington, Delaware, where she sold cakes, fruit, and desserts to wealthy people for their parties. Her son, Jeremiah Shadd, was a butcher, well-known for his ability to cure meat. His wife, known as Aunt Sallie Shadd, achieved legendary status among Wilmington's free black population as the inventor of ice cream. . . . Like other members of her family, she went into the catering business and created a new dessert sensation made from frozen cream, sugar, and fruit.[21]

Entrepreneurs such as Aunt Sallie Shadd were able to thrive in Delaware, one of the most prosperous of the thirteen colonies because of its small size, active shipping business, and fertile soil. The availability of free labor allowed the Three Lower Counties to grow throughout the eighteenth century. But when the Revolutionary War broke out in 1775, the peaceful life of sleepy Delawareans would be disrupted by fear, fighting, and bitter debate.

Chapter Four

Delaware During the Revolution

Delaware continued to grow throughout the eighteenth century. By 1770 there were more than thirty-seven thousand people in the Three Lower Counties. Most people were farmers or those who earned money in related agricultural fields such as grain milling, food production, leather tanning, shipbuilding, and exporting. The land was bountiful and some families had grown quite wealthy in the booming eighteenth-century economy. Most of Delaware's residents were second- or third-generation Americans who spoke "the king's English," and considered themselves to be part of a cultured and educated society.

Residents of Delaware found good company in the other twelve English colonies where 2 to 3 million people resided from New Hampshire, Massachusetts, Pennsylvania, and New York in the north to Georgia and the Carolinas in the south. The Americans in these colonies were generally hardworking and fiercely independent, having built a rich colonial power in little more than one hundred years.

The population of Great Britain was only twice that of the thirteen colonies, but the king of England and Parliament, the British legislature, held strict control over governmental, social, and business affairs in the thirteen colonies. These British overseers believed that the colonies existed only to benefit Great Britain. Though the colonists might have disagreed with this policy, Great Britain was the most powerful nation in the world in the eighteenth century, and its navy controlled the oceans from Europe to India.

The French and Indian War

As far as the English were concerned, the thirteen colonies were simply an extension of the British Empire and were expected to support policies and endeavors of the British government. This included financially supporting and fighting in a series of wars between Great Britain and France. These two eighteenth-century superpowers were locked in a continual power struggle over who would control Europe and who would profit by exploiting the New World. Beginning in 1693, England and France fought a series of four wars on the European continent, in America, and elsewhere.

In 1754, the French and Indian War broke out pitting Great Britain against France and their Native American allies. The war was fought primarily in New York, Pennsylvania, Ohio, and Canada, but French privateers plied the Delaware coast, striking fear into the populace when they stopped on occasion to plunder Lewes and other towns.

The French and Indian War ended in 1763 with the victorious British driving the French out of Canada and the western frontier of America. For the British, however, there was an unforeseen side effect to this victory: Without the French threatening the colonies, Americans no longer needed the British for protection. The English, however, felt that Americans should be eternally grateful to the motherland for saving their homes and property from the French.

Taxation Without Representation

The British government was near bankruptcy after the French and Indian War and was forced to double taxes on English farmers. And since Great Britain had defended the colonies, politicians in Parliament decided it was only fair for America to pay for its own defense. On March 22, 1765, Parliament passed the Stamp Act placing taxes on legal documents, newspapers, pamphlets, and even playing cards.

The Stamp Act created widespread outrage among the colonists, as described by Jane Harrington Scott in *A Gentleman as Well as a Whig:*

Colonists were outraged about the passage of the Stamp Act, a tax that Great Britain imposed to pay for the costs of the French and Indian War.

The Stamp Act was pervasive. It not only taxed business documents, such as newspapers, professional licenses, and ship clearances, but, by levying fees on diplomas, deeds, wills, and other personal legal documents, it adversely affected landholders, merchants, lawyers, judges and printers; men who had faithfully supported Britain in the French and Indian War. . . . All these men saw this tax as having little to do with foreign trade. Rather, it was a serious impediment to business within the colonies themselves; matters they considered to be well outside of Britain's jurisdiction. As loyal Englishmen, they felt profoundly betrayed.[22]

Resistance to the Stamp Act was found among rich and poor alike. It seemed that from the wealthiest planter to the humblest carpenter, there was widespread agreement that aristocrats in Great Britain had no right to levy taxes on Americans. Even in Delaware, where life was relatively easy and prosperous citizens were hardly prone to revolt, the Stamp Act caused an uproar, as Attorney General George Read mentioned in a 1765 letter to an English official:

The stamp-act you made on your side of the water hath raised such a ferment among us . . . that I know not when it will subside. . . . I sincerely wish the furious zeal of the populace may not be resented by your people in power as to prevent them from lending a candid ear to our just complaints. . . . If this law should stand unrepealed, or, indeed, any other enactment . . . imposing an internal tax . . . the colonists will entertain an opinion that they are to become the slaves of Great Britain.[23]

In October 1765, representatives from nine of the thirteen colonies met in New York at the Stamp Act Congress in order to coordinate resistance to the new tax. Delaware native Caesar Rodney, who had served as Kent County sheriff, a lower court judge, and a member of the Delaware assembly, was at the Stamp Act Congress. He was accompanied by Thomas McKean, a fellow

Delaware native Caesar Rodney attended the Stamp Act Congress in an effort to get the tax repealed.

assembly representative. Dover native and respected Philadelphia lawyer John Dickinson was also at the congress.

Dickinson is known as the "penman of the Revolution," because of his widely read newspaper articles written to oppose British policy in the colonies. His first well-regarded piece of revolutionary writing was the Stamp Act Resolution, signed by representatives at the Stamp Act Congress. While acknowledging the colony's debt to Great Britain, Dickinson's resolution stated that since Americans were not represented in Parliament, the British government had no right to levy taxes on the colonies. This concept, known as "taxation without representation," popularized by Massachusetts revolutionary James Otis, later formed the foundation of the American Revolution.

The American colonists had never before united to oppose British policies, and each man was risking his career and well-being by signing the resolution and taking a stand against the king. As Rodney wrote, signing the Stamp Act Resolution was "one of the most Difficult Tasks as I have ever yet . . . Undertaken, as We had Carefully to avoid any Infringement of the prerogative of the Crown, and the power of Parliament, and Yet in Duty bound fully to Assert the Rights & Privileges of the Colonies."[24]

Tea Taxes and a Boston Party

The Stamp Act proved to be a failure for British lawmakers. Stamp burnings and anti-stamp riots broke out in Lewes and elsewhere throughout the colonies. In addition there were widespread protests by government officials, and nearly all tax collectors assigned the job of selling the stamps resigned. On March 18, 1766, Parliament repealed the hated tax. Rodney and McKean were treated as heroes when they returned to the Delaware legislature in May 1766. During the session, McKean drafted a letter to the king thanking him in the most flattering terms for repealing the tax.

While people throughout the colonies celebrated, they conveniently ignored the "declaratory act" that accompanied the repeal, in which Parliament stated clearly that it had full power to make laws governing taxes in the colonies. Little more than a year later, in June 1767,

Philadelphia Influence

Although London was one of the largest cities in the world on the eve of the Revolution, Philadelphia was the second largest city in the British Empire. Philadelphia was an important city to the people of Delaware as most of the river traffic that passed through Delaware was traveling to or from the Pennsylvania capital. James A. Munroe writes about the tight bonds between Delaware and Philadelphia in History of Delaware:

It would be difficult to overemphasize the influence of Philadelphia on Delaware, for Philadelphia by 1775 dominated the economic and cultural life of the Delaware valley, its influence extending to Lewes, the home of Delaware River pilots, and to the St. Jones River and [elsewhere], where landings were loaded with produce bound for Philadelphia even more often than for New Castle and Wilmington. There was an area of southwestern Sussex where farmers had an easier commercial connection with the Chesapeake Bay than with the Delaware River, but even here the Philadelphia influence was not lacking....

If Philadelphians were upset by British revenue measures or by commercial restrictions, their fears were soon transmitted to Delaware. Tales of corruption in high places in Great Britain and suspicion of conspiracies against colonial well-being entered Delaware through the same channel.

Parliament enacted the Townshend Acts, taxes on glass, lead, paint, paper, and the favorite drink of colonists, tea.

Like the Stamp Act, this tax was universally denounced throughout the colonies. When the assembly of the Three Lower Counties met in 1768, they unanimously passed a resolution declaring that the Townshend Acts deprived colonial governments of the exclusive right to levy taxes upon its own citizens. Once again, Dickinson took pen in hand to oppose an act of Parliament, writing twelve articles that questioned Great Britain's right to tax Americans. These articles were known as the Farmer's Letters and were published over the course of two years in a Philadelphia newspaper.

Dickinson was joined by many other Americans who wrote pamphlets and articles opposing the colonial relationship to Great Britain. By 1770, the Townshend Acts were repealed, except for the tax on tea. The colonists reacted by organizing a boycott against tea, replacing their beloved drink with herbal drinks or coffee.

For three years, Americans protested the tea tax. In Virginia in March 1773, a legislator named Dabney Carr proposed the establishment of a Committee of Correspondence whose members would coordinate legislatures in each colony to offer a united

In December 1773, the Boston Tea Party took place when 150 men disguised as Native Americans dumped more than 300 chests of tea into Boston Harbor.

opposition to British policies. Rodney, McKean, and Read were appointed to sit on Delaware's Committee of Correspondence.

Events turned critical in December 1773, when several ships loaded with imported tea sailed into Boston harbor. On the night of December 16, about 150 men disguised as Native Americans boarded the ships and threw 352 chests of tea into the harbor. The Boston Tea Party, as the act came to be known, provoked Parliament to close the busy Boston port until the tea, valued today at over $1 million, was paid for. Parliament also disbanded the Massachusetts legislature and prohibited town meetings. These measures, called "the Intolerable Acts" by the Americans, were enforced by soldiers who began to drill in the streets of Boston in battle gear.

"An Invasion of Our Just Rights"

The Intolerable Acts prompted the people of Delaware to action. Meetings were held in all three of Delaware's county seats, attended by all voters in the area. Money was raised to help Bostonians affected by the economic hardship of the blockade, Committees of Correspondence were set up in each county, and resolutions were passed condemning British actions. One such resolution, passed at the Sussex County courthouse in July 1774, typified the feelings of the Delawareans, saying, "it is the inherent right of British subjects to be taxed by their own consent, or by representatives chosen by themselves only, and that every act of the British Parliament respecting our internal policy of North America, is unconstitutional, and an invasion of our just rights and privileges."[25]

On August 1, a convention was held in New Castle. Rodney, McKean, and Read were unanimously elected as delegates to the First Continental Congress to be held in Philadelphia in September. The purpose of the congress was to allow the colonies to unite in their resistance to the Intolerable Acts. It was agreed that the Delaware representatives would swear allegiance to the king, but protest the Boston blockade in the strongest possible terms and reassert the colonists' right to tax themselves.

During the congress, held between September 5 and October 26, the Delaware representatives debated weighty matters of colonial rights and security. They decided to protest by refusing to trade with England and boycotting all taxed British goods. After agreeing to meet again in May 1775 the Congress was adjourned. When Rodney, Read, and McKean reported back to the Delaware assembly, they were immediately appointed to attend the Second Continental Congress.

A Question of Loyalty

On April 19, 1775, less than a month before the Second Continental Congress was scheduled to meet, the first battles of the Revolutionary War were fought in Lexington and Concord, Massachusetts. Within a week, the news of war had been brought to New Castle by messengers on horseback. When the Second Continental Congress met again on May 10, there was solemn business to attend to, as James A. Munroe writes in *History of Delaware:*

> [The Congress] supported measures to create a Continental army commanded by [George] Washington, while a revolutionary committee system gradually put Delaware on a war footing—to the discomfiture of some citizens. Committees of observation and inspection supervised enforcement of the new boycott . . . while committees of safety began to gather arms and provide for military training.[26]

With the outbreak of war, the atmosphere in Delaware became charged with emotion. While some people supported a revolution, others feared that they would hang for treason unless they remained loyal to the British government. Violent disagreements broke out between neighbors and even within families.

Loyalties also divided along religious and cultural lines. The Scotch-Irish Presbyterians had a deep-seated hatred for the English because they felt their families had been mistreated when they lived in Ireland. But most of Delaware's people were of English descent and members of the Church of England. So while some Presbyterian ministers preached revolution from the pulpit and Scotch-Irish became some of the leading revolutionaries, Anglicans often prayed for reconciliation.

While some followed religious teachings, others opposed the revolution for monetary reasons, finding they could make handsome profits by selling tea and other goods that were part of the boycott. One such Delaware Loyalist was Thomas Robinson who sold forbidden tea in his shop.

To resist the revolutionaries, Robinson organized a group of fifteen hundred men from Sussex County to storm the garrison at Lewes and seize weapons and ammunition that might be used against the British. Robinson was arrested, but was later pardoned by the Delaware assembly. Robinson left the colonies on a British warship and did not return until the Revolution ended in 1781. As for the rest of the average citizens in the colony, Munroe writes:

The number of Delawareans so dissatisfied with the state of affairs as to participate actively in a war of rebellion was a minority, even of the free white inhabitants. Yet the number of loyalists so confirmed in their adherence to their [British] monarch . . . was apparently a smaller minority still. A significant number of the people were willing to allow themselves to be moved by events, day by day, to float with the American tide, causing little disturbance, accepting the inevitable. The rebels and the Tories [British loyalists] made the most noise. . . . But there was also a quieter element of humbler folk, like the Quakers and the Methodists, not to mention the more than 20 percent of the population who were black—a quiet element that cared little who won the war.

The happy situation of the Lower Counties as a semi-independent colony, an almost forgotten corner of the empire, plus the small size of the colony and the consequent limited ambitions for its development, produced a situation where a moderate course would seem safest.[27]

The First Naval Battle

Although some advocated moderation, many men were ready to fight the British and loosely organized militias formed throughout the Three Lower Counties. Rodney was elected colonel of one regiment, and according to Scott, he signed a written oath, "to defend liberties and privileges of America at risk to [his] own [life] and fortunes."[28]

By September, about five thousand men in Delaware had offered their services to the Continental army. Some fought the British in New York while others were kept busy fortifying the Delaware River against English warships.

In March 1776, the first of those ships, the heavily armed English man-of-war, *Roebuck*, sailed into Delaware Bay. While the militia quickly marched from New Castle in order to protect Lewes, the *Roebuck* sailed by without incident.

On May 8, the first naval battle of the Revolutionary War was fought when the *Roebuck* sailed up the river to Wilmington accompanied by a small warship called the *Liverpool*. This so frightened the local citizens that they loaded their furniture, clothing, and other possessions on wagons and fled into the woods. Meanwhile the Wilmington militia filed into fourteen long rowboats with mounted guns called row-galleys, and began loading them with ammunition.

When the British warships reached Christina River, a battle ensued and bullets and cannonballs flew for more than three hours. Thousands of Wilmington citizens assembled on the riverbanks to watch the action.

As night fell, the *Roebuck* tried to sail closer to the galleys and ran aground in the shallow water at the mouth of the creek. The boat listed, causing its mounted cannons to become useless, and the *Liverpool* was forced to sail nearby to protect the trapped ship until darkness ended the battle. The next day, the rising tide freed the ship, but it was chased off by the Americans. The great British warships finally limped off to be repaired, defeated by Continental militiamen in row-galleys. One American was killed, however, and two were wounded.

Becoming a State

Meanwhile, the idea of separating from England was growing in popularity. In January 1776, a pamphlet called *Common Sense*, written by Thomas Paine, was published in the colonies. The booklet, which advocated complete independence from England, sold over 100,000 copies in less than three months—an American sales record that would not be broken for several centuries. Suddenly the word independence began to appear in newspapers and was loudly proclaimed at street rallies and protests. But support for independence was hardly universal. People in New York, Maryland, and Virginia, for instance, were more dependent on British trade than other colonies and so did not want to break with the mother country. And Quakers were against any war, no matter how just the cause.

These concerns were on the minds of the colonial delegates when they met in Philadelphia in June 1776, for the meeting of the Continental Congress. As in the rest of the country, there was division within the Delaware assembly. Rodney and McKean were strongly in favor of seeking independence while Read did not think a ragtag army of Americans could defeat the British Empire.

In 1776, Thomas Paine wrote *Common Sense*, a pamphlet that championed complete independence from England.

By the end of June, the delegates were ready to vote on the Declaration of Independence, written by Thomas Jefferson. As colonel of a militia regiment, however, Rodney was in Delaware putting down a loyalist uprising. As the time to vote drew near, McKean realized that without Rodney, the Delaware vote would not count because it would be split between himself and Read, who could not be convinced to vote for independence.

To break the tie, McKean sent a messenger to explain the situation to Rodney, who proceeded to ride his horse eighty miles without

COMMON SENSE;

ADDRESSED TO THE

INHABITANTS

OF

AMERICA,

On the following interesting

SUBJECTS.

I. Of the Origin and Design of Government in general, with concise Remarks on the English Constitution.

II. Of Monarchy and Hereditary Succession.

III. Thoughts on the present State of American Affairs.

IV. Of the present Ability of America, with some miscellaneous Reflections.

A NEW EDITION, with several Additions in the Body of the Work. To which is added an APPENDIX; together with an Address to the People called QUAKERS.

N. B. The New Addition here given increases the Work upwards of one Third.

Man knows no Master save creating HEAVEN,
Or those whom Choice and common Good ordain.
THOMSON.

resting from Dover to Philadelphia. Meanwhile McKean made speeches to delay the vote. Finally, as the vote was being taken, Rodney arrived. Seeing he was outnumbered within the delegation, Read finally changed his mind. The Declaration of Independence, signed by Rodney, Read, and McKean, was formally adopted on July 4, 1776.

In September a convention was held in New Castle to write a constitution for Delaware. No longer called a colony of England, or the Three Lower Counties, Delaware was now an independent state. The position of governor was replaced by a president, who was appointed by the assembly and shared power with a four-man council. The legal document written to govern Delaware was the first constitution drawn up by any state in America.

Battle of Cooch's Bridge

On May 12, 1777, the capital of Delaware was moved from New Castle to Dover. A few months later, Delaware would see its first— and only—land battle in the Revolution.

Capturing Delaware was not the goal of British General William Howe. The peninsula simply lay between his 260 heavily armed ships on the Atlantic and the capital city of Philadelphia. Howe had attempted to march his fifteen thousand well-equipped and highly trained soldiers to Philadelphia but was repulsed by Washington's army at Trenton and Princeton, New Jersey. Instead the British general turned around and captured New York City.

Citizens of Delaware grew alarmed in July when Howe's warships, schooners, and tenders were seen off the Delaware coast. Although the Delawareans expected the British to sail up the Delaware to Philadelphia, Howe reasoned that the bay and river were too well-fortified and well-defended. By August, the Americans realized that Howe intended to take Philadelphia by land after first sailing up to the northernmost part of Chesapeake Bay and then marching overland.

Luck was on the side of the Americans. The hot August weather was so calm that there was little wind to drive Howe's fleet, and it took the British more than three weeks—until August 25—to reach their destination. Nevertheless, Howe's forces were able to disembark unopposed near Elkton at the northern edge of the Chesapeake.

Meanwhile, Washington had moved an army of ten thousand men from Philadelphia and New York to Wilmington. Rodney was ordered by John McKinly, president of Delaware, to take his regiment "to such Places as may be most necessary to annoy the Enemy & prevent them from effecting their purpose."[29]

In order to thwart the British invasion, Washington ordered his ragtag army to spread out in a long east-west line from Newport, Delaware, south of Wilmington, on into Pennsylvania. The American general sent William Maxwell with 720 light infantry troops to the woods near Glasgow, on the Maryland border east of Howe's position in Elkton.

General William Maxwell led 720 colonists in the Battle of Cooch's Bridge, a conflict that ended in defeat for the Americans.

Howe's army pushed into Delaware, along the Newark-Glasgow Road, and on the morning of September 3, they met Maxwell's troops who were hiding in the woods. A battle ensued near a creek crossing named Cooch's Bridge. The outgunned and outnumbered Americans were forced to retreat, losing forty soldiers at what is now known as the Battle of Cooch's Bridge. The British burned a local mill to the ground and seized the public records and monies from a local courthouse.

After the battle, in a stunning defeat for the Americans, the British captured Wilmington, arresting Delaware president John McKinly and seizing the state treasury along with many public records. Leaving behind the sick and wounded, and an occupying army, Howe continued on to Philadelphia where he set up headquarters while members of the Continental Congress fled the city. Meanwhile, having captured Wilmington, the British naval fleet was able to sail up the Delaware River to Philadelphia unopposed.

The British did not occupy the rest of Delaware but there was fear that the enemy could overrun the state at any time. Nevertheless, government functions continued and in McKinly's absence, Read and McKean served briefly as acting governors. Then, as Munroe writes:

> At that dangerous time, when it took unusual courage and devotion to the cause of independence to be chief executive of a state that was without a Treasury and threatened at any moment by British naval power, the assembly chose Caesar Rodney as the second elected president.[30]

Serving with Honor

Fears of a British takeover of Delaware were alleviated when the Continental army dealt the British a bitter defeat in Saratoga, New York, in October 1777. The British in New York had been expecting assistance from Howe's army, who had taken so long to capture Philadelphia they could not lend their support. This military defeat caused Howe to resign in disgrace, and the British were soon forced to abandon Philadelphia while their naval fleet relinquished control of the Delaware River.

The citizens of Delaware were able to return to peace. Delaware soldiers, however, were to continue fighting in the revolution as they had done from the beginning. Early in the war, Delaware soldiers fought side by side with George Washington and saw battle in New York, Pennsylvania, and elsewhere. In fact, the Delaware regiment led by Robert Kirkwood made such a reputation for itself fighting in the Carolinas that they were known as "Blue Hen's Chickens" for the tough, dark-blue gamecocks bred in Kent County. That nickname is still used to identify Delawareans.

After the British ended their occupation of Philadelphia and Wilmington in 1778, the war moved into the southern colonies, and the First Delaware Regiment fought in most of the battles. They

In 1781, British general Charles Cornwallis (left) surrendered to George Washington (right) and the American forces in Yorktown, Virginia.

were at Yorktown, Virginia, on October 19, 1781, to help defeat British general Charles Cornwallis. After Cornwallis surrendered his eight thousand troops, the Americans were the winners of the Revolutionary War.

During the war, Delaware furnished more troops in proportion to its population than any other colony. The First Delaware Regiment marched a total of five thousand miles between 1780 and 1783 when they returned home. Hundreds died in extremely harsh conditions from battle wounds, disease, and other deprivations. Like other Americans who fought in the Revolution, they were fighting for the ideals of self-government and freedom of thought and action.

Chapter Five

After Independence

When colonial representatives declared their independence from Great Britain in 1776, they faced many problems; the potential success of the new nation was hardly guaranteed. The cost of fighting the war was bankrupting state governments, raising taxes was a contentious issue, and there was little coordination between the states at a national level. The men who ran Delaware and the other colonies agreed that some sort of constitutional government was needed so that the states could function together as a unified country, yet maintain their individual sovereignty.

The Second Continental Congress met to take up these issues in 1777, when they drafted the first constitution of the United States, known as the Articles of Confederation. At that time they had assigned Delaware native John Dickinson (who had first made a name for himself by writing the Stamp Act Resolution in 1765) to head the committee to write the document.

Although Dickinson preferred a strong federal government with the authority to levy taxes, many other delegates feared an autocratic centralized government. Large states were afraid that they would pay a disproportionate amount of taxes to support such a governing entity and small states feared being dominated by more populous regions. With no central authority, however, the states continually bickered over control of western lands, trade restrictions, state court decisions, and a host of other complicated legal questions.

These disagreements were not resolved, but the Articles of Confederation were approved by ten of the thirteen colonies in 1778, with New Jersey, Delaware, and Maryland refusing to ratify the document. Every colony needed to sign on, however, so the articles were not formally adopted until the end of the Revolution. Munroe explains why Delaware was reluctant to join the other colonies:

> States like Delaware that had no claims to lands west of the Appalachian Mountains feared that large states with extensive claims, such as Virginia, in particular, would have overwhelming influence in the new government. To [Delaware and the others] it seemed that unsettled western lands ought to belong to the union as a whole.[31]

Weaknesses in the Articles of Confederation

Although the articles were never changed, Virginia ceded western lands to the federal government, influencing Delaware and New Jersey to ratify the Articles of Confederation in 1779. (Maryland, however, refused to do so until 1781.)

The articles created a loose central government with a single house of Congress in which each state had one vote. Congress was authorized to set up a postal department, request donations from states for taxes, raise an army, print money or borrow it as necessary, and control development in the western territories. The governing body could also declare war and sign treaties with foreign nations.

There were several weaknesses with the Articles of Con-federation, however, which led to serious national problems after the war was won. There was no president or federal judiciary to settle disagreements between the states, and Congress had no power to regulate trade or force citizens to pay taxes. Meanwhile states were refusing to provide tax dollars to the federal government and they were continually inciting trade wars, which were nearly destroying the national economy. As Munroe writes: "This weakness was particularly upsetting to Delaware, for it saw its commerce controlled by Pennsylvania, which could collect tariff duties on goods entering the port of Philadelphia even though destined to be sold in Delaware."[32]

In addition to these problems, the federal government had no funds to pay soldiers who had fought so bravely in the Revolutionary War, nor did it have money to pay suppliers who provided the soldiers' food and other basic necessities. When congressional delegates complained, they were widely ignored by state governments.

The Constitutional Convention

Hoping to alleviate some of the economic problems of the states, the Virginia legislature proposed a convention in Annapolis, Maryland, in September 1786. John Dickinson attended, but only five colonies were repre-sented. The small group accomplished little, but proposed that another convention be held in Phila-delphia in the spring, at which time all problems facing the new nation could be discussed.

On May 25, 1787, five representatives from Dela-ware including George Read and John Dickinson attended the Philadelphia meeting, known as the Constitutional Conven-tion. As a represent-ative from one of the smallest states in the union, Read was determined to ensure that Delaware was granted powers equal to New York, Massachusetts, Virginia, and other dominant states. Meanwhile Dickinson was concerned that the Articles of Confederation that he had helped draft were terribly flawed, so he proposed scrapping the entire document to write a new constitution.

George Read, who represented Delaware at the Constitutional Convention, was in favor of eliminating the Articles of Confederation and drafting a brand new constitution.

As the meeting opened, Virginia delegates presented a plan in which congressional representation would be based upon a state's population. With about 8 percent of Virginia's popu-lation, this meant that Delaware would only have one representative for every twelve from Virginia. The Delaware contingent strongly disagreed with this proposal and vowed not to sign any such measure.

As a compromise, the Constitutional Convention decided to form two governing bodies, a House of Representatives, in which delegates were elected in accordance with population numbers, and a Senate, with two representatives from each state. Although Delawareans would still be outnumbered in Congress, the delegates realized that it was the best situation they could hope for. After this problem was resolved, the five Delaware delegates supported nearly every other measure of the Constitution, including the creation of the judicial and executive branches of government.

The First State

By early August the first draft of the Constitution had been completed, and on September 17 it was signed by thirty-nine of the forty-two delegates present including all five from Delaware. Weary from weeks of bitter debate, the Delaware representatives returned home.

Before the Constitution could be adopted, each state had to assemble a special convention to ratify the document. At the next meeting of the Delaware assembly, the state president, Thomas Collins, read the Constitution and recommended it "as a subject of the most important consideration, involving in its adoption not only our prosperity and felicity, but perhaps our national existence."[33]

The state legislators decided to hold a special election on November 26, 1787, in which each county would pick ten men to attend a ratifying convention. When the thirty elected representatives finally voted in Dover on December 7, the delegates were unanimous in their approval. Thus Delaware be-came the first to ratify the U.S. Constitution and earned the nickname "First State."

After approving the Con-stitution, state representative James Tilton wrote:

> Although every other means under Providence should fail us . . . we hope at least to derive some consolation from the New Federal Constitu-tion. From hence we may expect some standing institutions to walk by. Fraudulent retrospective

laws will be no more. . . . And although it should be long, before Virtue shall become triumphant over Vice, good men will nevertheless be more out of the reach and power of unjust and wicked oppressors than Heretofore.[34]

In the weeks after ratification, the Delaware legislature chose George Read and Richard Bassett as representatives to the U.S. Senate and John Vining to the House of Representatives.

After the ratification of the Constitution, the Delaware legislature chose Richard Bassett as a representative to the U.S. Senate.

Dickinson Promotes the Constitution

In the two weeks after Delaware's approval of the Constitution, Pennsylvania and New Jersey also ratified the document. People in other states, however, were not as happy with the Constitution because they felt it failed to protect individual rights such as freedom of speech and the right to trial by jury. In addition, New York and Virginia, the two most populous states in the Union, were locked in contentious debates over other divisive issues.

In early 1788, Dickinson became alarmed that all the states had not accepted the Constitution. To motivate state legislators into action, Dickinson wrote a series of anonymous letters urging ratification of the Constitution. Much like his renowned Farmer's Letters published before the revolution, the *Fabius Letters*, were published in newspapers throughout the country and were credited with influencing popular opinion. In an article from *Humanitas* magazine, Gregory S. Ahern explains the meaning behind the name used by the author:

Dickinson's choice of pseudonym sets the tone for his letters. . . . Quintus Fabius Maximus Cunctator was the Roman general who saved the republic through caution, prudence, patience, and persistence. Indeed, the *Fabius Letters* are a model of moderation and prudence, with their frequent appeals to history to justify the new Constitution and to warn against the danger to the nation should it fail to be ratified.[35]

By the summer of 1788, Virginia and New York had ratified the Constitution. When a Bill of Rights was proposed in the 1789 Congress, North Carolina followed, and Rhode Island became the last state to ratify on May 29, 1790. The independent states were now united, and Dickinson penned the inspirational words:

Delightful are the prospects that will open to the view of United America—her sons well prepared to defend their own happiness, and ready to relieve the misery of others—her fleets formidable, but only to the unjust—her revenue sufficient, yet unoppressive—her commerce affluent, but not debasing—peace and plenty within her borders—and the glory that arises from a proper use of power, encircling them.[36]

A New Constitution

Delaware had been the first state after independence to write its own constitution. Now, with the federal Constitution approved, legislators began work on a new state constitution to fix problems with the original document that had been quickly written in 1776 and approved during the uncertain days of the Revolution.

On November 29, the Delaware constitutional convention opened in Dover. Delegates made some small changes such as renaming two houses of the General Assembly the House of Representatives and the Senate. The title of the state's chief executive officer was changed from president to governor, and the men elected to that role were given greater powers to appoint judges and other officials.

Restrictions were put on who could serve in the legislature. For instance, any man serving as senator had to be at least twenty-seven years old and a resident of the state for at least three years. A senator was also expected to be a man of wealth as the constitution required him to own at least two thousand acres of property or a business worth £1000.

The new constitution established three branches of the state court and eased voting restrictions. New voters only needed to pay taxes to qualify, not own extensive landholdings or businesses. Since every man in Delaware was charged a small tax every year, this made voting more democratic, allowing even poor men to vote. But the new constitution expressly prevented women and blacks from voting, which was also the case in the other twelve colonies.

Mirroring the federal Bill of Rights, religious freedom was included in the new Delaware state constitution which stated that no person could be denied public office because of his religion. This allowed Catholics and Jews, who had previously faced discrimination, to run for office.

Washington's Approval

When John Dickinson published the Fabius Letters promoting ratification of the Constitution, George Washington wrote a letter to a friend expressing his appreciation for the Delawarean's writing skills. Washington's letter, quoted in Gregory S. Ahern, "The Spirit of American Constitutionalism: John Dickinson's Fabius Letters," read:

I must beg you to accept my best thanks for your polite attention in forwarding [The Fabius Letters] to me. The writer of those pieces, signed Fabius, whoever he is, appears to be master of his subject; he treats it with dignity, and at the same time expresses himself in such manner as to render it intelligible to every capacity. I have no doubt but that an extensive republication of those [letters] would be of utility in removing the impressions which have been made upon the minds of many by an unfair or partial representation of the proposed constitution, and would afford desirable information upon the subject to those who sought for it.

With these new constitutional provisions, Delaware allowed a greater percentage of its people to vote in elections than any other state in the Union.

Slavery's Slow Decline

The new constitution, while not specifically outlawing slavery, let stand several laws, such as the ban on the importation of slaves from other states, that discouraged slavery. There was also a law forbidding the exportation of slaves to other states, and slaves who were illegally brought into Delaware were granted immediate freedom. As Munroe writes, "these laws . . . had practically banned the interstate slave trade from Delaware and in doing so contributed to the decline of slavery there."[37]

Since nearly half the 757,000 slaves in America lived in Maryland and Virginia, Delaware was surrounded by states where slavery was well entrenched. If Delaware had allowed the interstate trading of slaves, a city such as New Castle might have held one of the largest slave markets in the United States.

Although this did not happen, slavery remained legal in Delaware, and according to the first census taken in 1790, there were eighty-nine hundred slaves living among the state's fifty-nine thousand people, meaning slaves made up about 15 percent of the total population. And the brutalities of slavery were well documented within Delaware's borders. For example, in 1781, a black woman named Sabrina was whipped to death by her master in public at Wilmington's Christina Bridge. The farmer who committed this crime was charged with manslaughter but later acquitted.

Such horrors only strengthened the resolve of those who wanted to end slavery. In 1788, Quakers formed the Delaware Society for Promoting the Abolition of Slavery. This powerful group spoke out about the immorality of slavery, protected free blacks from being kidnapped and sold into slavery in the South, and also helped runaway slaves escape to the North.

With a strong belief in the power of education to improve the lives of former slaves, the Quakers opened a school for blacks in Wilmington in 1798. In 1816, a Quaker group known as the African School Society opened another. These schools taught religion and reading and encouraged young boys to learn farming or become blacksmiths, carpenters, and shoemakers. Girls were taught domestic arts such as sewing, food preparation, and gardening.

Blacks were also invited to Quaker and Methodist religious services and some parishioners were inspired to start their own churches. For example, the Ezion Methodist Episcopal Church in Wilmington became the first black church in Delaware in 1805. By 1843, the congregation listed more than twelve hundred members.

Religious, economic, and social factors continued to reduce the number of slaves in Delaware. By 1820 there were fewer than forty-five hundred slaves in the state and by 1840 the number of blacks held in slavery had dropped to 13 percent of the total black population of Delaware.

A Growing Industrial Power

The decline of slavery can also be attributed to the fact that Delaware was becoming a manufacturing center while moving away from the traditional agricultural economy. After the Revolution, the waterpower provided by the rapid fall of the Brandywine River allowed Wilmington to stand at the center of a booming milling and transportation hub. Delaware and Pennsylvania farmers could turn their grain into flour at the city's sixty mills before shipping it around the world.

Grain was often brought to the mills by Conestoga wagons that traveled from southeastern Pennsylvania in groups of twenty or thirty. As Peter C. Welsh writes in *Readings in Delaware History:* "Often these wagons congested streets for blocks at a time, while the confusion of wheels, animals, and drivers created bedlam as they waited their turn to come up beside a mill to be unloaded."[38]

After the Revolution, other waterpower industries began building along the banks of the Brandywine, including two tobacco snuff mills. In addition, Welsh writes there were "six sawmills, a paper mill ... [and] a barley mill, giving employment to over one hundred people and indirectly supporting scores of coopers [barrel makers], blacksmiths, weavers, cotton card makers, carpenters, and millwrights."[39]

These businesses created a great demand for ships; over thirty large, square-rigged ships operated out of Wilmington's port. With direct access to the open sea, via Delaware Bay, the grain-laden ships plied the seas between the West Indies and Europe. On their return journeys to America, the ships were laden with European wines, chocolates, fine clothing, books, furniture, and other imported goods that allowed Wilmington's prosperous citizens to take pleasure in the finest products the world had to offer.

Gunpowder and Iron

In 1800, Delaware's most prominent family began its long Delaware legacy when Eleuthere Irenee du Pont moved to Wilmington and founded the E. I. du Pont de Nemours & Company, or the Du Pont Company. Du Pont came from a family of French citizens prominent in political and military affairs who fled to Wilmington to escape the chaos that followed the French Revolution in the late eighteenth century.

Du Pont was a scientist who specialized in the manufacture of high-quality gunpowder and began manufacturing the substance at a place he called Eleutherian Mills. According to Munroe, du Pont chose this site because

> it had a constant, dependable flow of water to work the mills; it was close to navigable rivers, which allowed importation of needed materials, like saltpeter and sulphur, and exportation of the finished product; and it lay at a distance from a city, explosions being a constant threat in the powder business and capable of doing especially severe damage if the powder works were located where population was concentrated.[40]

Du Pont's father was well known in diplomatic circles and was friends with President Thomas Jefferson, who readily agreed to let the Du Pont Company supply the U.S. military with gunpowder. By 1811, du Pont was the largest manufacturer of gunpowder in America.

Iron manufacture was also an important industry in Delaware. There were more than five iron forges in Sussex County that utilized the coal from nearby Pennsylvania to produce metal. The iron was

By 1811, E. I. du Pont's gunpowder mill in Delaware was the largest producer of gunpowder in America.

rolled into sheets and cut at steel mills in New Castle, and turned into nails and iron bars in Wilmington.

With so many firms, factories, and mills scattered throughout the three counties of Delaware, transportation of goods became increasingly important, and enterprises were formed to build roads and bridges across the state. Construction companies built bridges across the Brandywine, Christina, and other rivers, and graded new roads throughout the state. These roads were called turnpikes because a toll was charged to each wagon that used the road. After the toll was paid, a bar, known as a pikestaff, was raised to allow the wagon to continue.

In the two centuries after Henry Hudson sailed into Delaware Bay, Delaware was forever changed from a heavily forested peninsula dominated by the forces of nature, to a populated agricultural and industrial center ruled by men, machines, and money. The original Lenape inhabitants of the state left the area as a series of rulers from the Netherlands, Sweden, England, and the United States put their permanent stamp on Delaware's three counties.

The citizens of Delaware have been flourishing since Dutch colonists first built their settlements along the Christina. After the American Revolution, Delawareans had enough optimism and foresight to become the first state to ratify the Constitution. From its proud beginnings, the Diamond State has set a shining example of liberty and freedom that continues to this day.

Notes

Chapter One: First Contact

1. Quoted in Jeanette Eckman, *Delaware: A Guide to the First State*. New York: Hastings House, 1955, p. 3.
2. Hitakonanu'laxk (Tree Beard), *The Grandfathers Speak: Native American Folk Tales of the Lenapé People*. New York: Interlink Books, 1994, pp. 9–10.
3. Quoted in Henry Hudson, *Henry Hudson the Navigator*. New York: Burt Franklin, n. d. Reprint of the 1855 edition, pp. 168–69.
4. Quoted in Harry Emerson Wildes, *The Delaware*. New York: Farrar & Rinehart, 1940, p. 15.
5. Wildes, *The Delaware*, p. 20.
6. James A. Munroe, *Colonial Delaware—A History*. Millwood, NY: KTO Press, 1978, pp. 7–8.
7. Quoted in Munroe, *Colonial Delaware—A History*, p. 8.
8. Munroe, *Colonial Delaware—A History*, p. 9.

Chapter Two: European Settlement

9. C. A. Weslager, *New Sweden on the Delaware: 1638-1655*. Wilmington, DE: Middle Atlantic Press, 1988, pp. 36–37.
10. Quoted in Israel Acrelius, *A History of New Sweden*. Ann Arbor, MI: University Microfilms, 1966, pp. 26–27.
11. Quoted in Acrelius, *A History of New Sweden*, p. 39.
12. Acrelius, *A History of New Sweden*, p. 79.
13. Eckman, *Delaware: A Guide to the First State*, p. 31.
14. Quoted in Anna T. Lincoln, *Wilmington, Delaware: Three Centuries Under Four Flags*. Rutland, VT: Tuttle Publishing, 1937, p. 47.
15. Eckman, *Delaware: A Guide to the First State*, p. 35.

Chapter Three: Daily Life in Colonial Delaware

16. Quoted in Carol E. Hoffecker, ed., *Readings in Delaware History*. Newark: University of Delaware Press, 1973, p. 10.
17. James A. Munroe, *History of Delaware*. Newark: University of Delaware Press, 1993, pp. 40–41.
18. Quoted in Hoffecker, *Readings in Delaware History*, p. 30.

19. Quoted in Hoffecker, *Readings in Delaware History*, p. 31.

20. Quoted in Hoffecker, *Readings in Delaware History*, p. 37.

21. Carol Hoffecker and Annette Woolard, "Black Women in Delaware's History," August 4, 1997. www.udel.edu/BlackHistory/blackwomen.html.

Chapter Four: Delaware During the Revolution

22. Jane Harrington Scott, *A Gentleman as Well as a Whig*. Newark: University of Delaware Press, 2000, p. 31.

23. Quoted in Scott, *A Gentleman as Well as a Whig*, p. 33.

24. Quoted in Scott, *A Gentleman as Well as a Whig*, p. 35.

25. Quoted in Scott, *A Gentleman as Well as a Whig*, p. 157.

26. Munroe, *History of Delaware*, p. 66.

27. Munroe, *History of Delaware*, pp. 62–63.

28. Scott, *A Gentleman as Well as a Whig*, p. 87.

29. Quoted in Scott, *A Gentleman as Well as a Whig*, p. 157.

30. Munroe, *History of Delaware*, p. 75.

Chapter Five: After Independence

31. Munroe, *History of Delaware*, p. 77.

32. Munroe, *History of Delaware*, p. 78.

33. Quoted in Hoffecker, *Readings in Delaware History*, p. 75.

34. Quoted in Hoffecker, *Readings in Delaware History*, p. 76.

35. Gregory S. Ahern, "The Spirit of American Constitutionalism: John Dickinson's *Fabius Letters*," April 8, 2000. www.nhinet.org/ahern.htm.

36. Quoted in Ahern, "The Spirit of American Constitutionalism."

37. Munroe, *History of Delaware*, p. 84.

38. Quoted in Hoffecker, *Readings in Delaware History*, p. 87.

39. Quoted in Hoffecker, *Readings in Delaware History*, p. 83.

40. Munroe, *History of Delaware*, p. 105.

Chronology

1609
Henry Hudson sails into Delaware Bay.

1610
Sir Samuel Argall sails his ship into Delaware Bay to escape a storm. He names it after the governor of Virginia, Sir Thomas West, third Baron De La Warr.

1625
The Dutch West India Company builds a settlement on the site of present-day New York City and calls it New Amsterdam.

1630
The first official land acquisition in Delaware is registered by the governor of New Netherlands.

1631
Dutch settlers begin to build a settlement at Zwannendael (Valley of the Swans).

1632
David de Vries discovers that the settlers at Zwannendael had been massacred some months earlier.

1638
Peter Minuit and about seventy Swedish colonists settle New Sweden near present-day Wilmington.

1643
John "Big Belly" Printz becomes governor of New Sweden.

1655
The Dutch seize New Sweden and take control of the Delaware River.

1664
The English seize New Amsterdam from the Dutch and rename it New York. In September, Delaware is also made a colony of Great Britain.

1682
The duke of York gives Delaware to William Penn, who makes it part of Pennsylvania.

1701
William Penn grants the Three Lower Counties the right to elect their own legislative assembly, independent from Pennsylvania's governing body.

1704
Delaware's first elected assembly meets in New Castle.

1763

The French are driven out of North America as Great Britain wins the French and Indian War.

1765

The Stamp Act placing a tax on paper goods is passed by the British Parliament, setting a course for revolution in the colonies.

1766

Parliament repeals the Stamp Act.

1767

Parliament enacts the Townshend Acts, taxes on glass, paper, lead, paint, and tea.

1773

The Boston Tea Party is held in which tax protesters dump $1 million worth of English tea into Boston harbor.

1774

Rodney, McKean, and George Read attend the First Continental Congress.

1775

The first battles of the Revolutionary War are fought in Lexington and Concord, Massachusetts.

1776

The first naval battle of the Revolutionary War is fought near Christina Creek as the English warships *Roebuck* and *Liverpool* are defeated by American soldiers in row-galleys; the Declaration of Independence is signed by all members of the Second Continental Congress in Philadelphia.

1777

The capital of Delaware is moved from New Castle to Dover; the Battle of Cooch's Bridge, the only Revolutionary War engagement in Delaware, is fought near the Maryland border; British forces capture New Castle, arrest Delaware president John McKinly, and seize treasury and public records.

1779

Delaware approves the Articles of Confederation.

1781

The Americans win the Revolutionary War when British general Charles Cornwallis surrenders at Yorktown, Virginia.

1787

Five representatives from Delaware attend the Constitutional Convention in Philadelphia and participate in the writing of the U.S. Constitution; Delaware becomes the first state to ratify the U.S. Constitution.

1788

Delaware Quakers form the Delaware Society for Promoting the Abolition of Slavery.

1792

Representatives meet in Dover to write a new state constitution.

For Further Reading

Jean F. Blashfield, *Delaware*. New York: Childrens Press, 2000. The geography, history, government, economy, and culture of Delaware for young adults, from the America the Beautiful series.

Ruth Dean and Melissa Thompson, *Life in the American Colonies*. San Diego: Lucent Books, 1999. An exploration of the day-to-day lives of settlers, manufacturers, farmers, slaves, and others in the American colonies from The Way People Live series.

William Dudley, *Opposing Viewpoints in American History*, vol. 1. San Diego: Greenhaven Press, 1996. Issues and events in American history from early exploration and settlement in the New World to the aftermath of the Civil War.

Dennis B. Fradin, *The Delaware Colony*. Chicago: Childrens Press, 1992. The origins and history of colonial Delaware from the time of the Lenape through Dutch rule, English rule, and the Revolutionary War.

Robert S. Grumet, *The Lenapes*. New York: Chelsea House, 1989. The culture, history, and daily lives of the Lenape who lived in Delaware and other Middle Atlantic states before European settlement.

Hitakonanu'laxk (Tree Beard), *The Grandfathers Speak: Native American Folk Tales of the Lenapé People*. New York: Interlink Books, 1994. The history of the Lenape people with traditional tales that make up the basis of the tribe's oral history.

Bonnie L. Lukes, *Colonial America*. San Diego: Lucent Books, 2000. Settlement and life in the original thirteen English colonies in North America.

Works Consulted

Books

Israel Acrelius, *A History of New Sweden.* Ann Arbor, MI: University Microfilms, 1966. A history of the Swedish colony in Delaware from its origins in 1638 to the middle of the 1700s, first published in 1759.

Jeanette Eckman, *Delaware: A Guide to the First State.* New York: Hastings House, 1955. Originally compiled by the Federal Writers' Project of the Works Progress Administration during the Great Depression, and extensively updated by the author in later years, the first half of this book is an in-depth look at the state of Delaware, the second half offers scenic and historic routes for tourists.

Sydney G. Fisher, *The Quaker Colonies.* New York: The United States Publishers Association, 1919. The history of the Pennsylvania and Delaware colonies from the time William Penn began settlement in the 1680s until the time of the Revolutionary War.

Carol E. Hoffecker, ed., *Readings in Delaware History.* Newark: University of Delaware Press, 1973. Historic articles about Delaware written by early settlers, politicians, ministers, and others from the time of the first settlement in the seventeenth century until the 1920s.

Henry Hudson, *Henry Hudson the Navigator.* New York: Burt Franklin, n.d. Reprint of the 1855 edition. The notes of Henry Hudson's three voyages to the Americas between 1607 and 1609, consisting mostly of technical navigation notes but with several interesting observations about the terrain and the Native Americans who lived there.

Anna T. Lincoln, *Wilmington, Delaware: Three Centuries Under Four Flags.* Rutland, VT: Tuttle Publishing, 1937. The history of Wilmington and Delaware under the rule of the Swedish, Dutch, English, and American governments written by the curator of the Historical Society of Delaware.

James A. Munroe, *Colonial Delaware—A History*. Millwood, NY: KTO Press, 1978. A detailed history of Delaware from the time of the first European settlement until the Revolutionary War, written by a professor and historian who is the author of several books about Delaware.

James A. Munroe, *History of Delaware*. Newark: University of Delaware Press, 1993. A book about the social, political, religious, and cultural history of Delaware.

Albert Cook Myers, ed., *Narratives of Early Pennsylvania, West New Jersey and Delaware, 1630–1707*. New York: Barnes & Noble, 1959. A book of source documents written by governors, sailors, ships' captains, clergymen, merchants, and other early settlers.

Jane Harrington Scott, *A Gentleman as Well as a Whig*. Newark: University of Delaware Press, 2000. A book about the life and times of Caesar Rodney, delegate to the First Continental Congress, signer of the Declaration of Independence, and president of Delaware from 1778 to 1781.

C. A. Weslager, *New Sweden on the Delaware: 1638–1655*. Wilmington, DE: Middle Atlantic Press, 1988. A detailed history of the Swedish colony in Delaware that lasted less than twenty years in the seventeenth century.

Harry Emerson Wildes, *The Delaware*. New York: Farrar & Rinehart, 1940. An interesting book about the history of the Delaware River from the time Henry Hudson first sailed it in 1609 until the early twentieth century.

Internet Sources

Gregory S. Ahern, "The Spirit of American Constitutionalism: John Dickinson's *Fabius Letters*," April 8, 2000. www.nhinet.org/ahern.htm. A 1998 article from *Humanitas* magazine about John Dickinson's letters written to support the ratification of the U.S. Constitution.

John Dickinson, "Stamp Act Congress—1765," Independence Hall Association in Philadelphia. July 4, 1995. www.ushistory.org/declaration/related/sac65.htm. A letter sent to the king of England opposing the Stamp Act of 1765.

Carol Hoffecker and Annette Woolard, "Black Women in Delaware's History," August 4, 1997. www.udel.edu/BlackHistory/blackwomen.html. Interesting details pertaining to the lives of black women in Delaware from the earliest settlement to the twentieth century.

Index

Index

Picture Credits

Cover photo: Permanent collection of University of Delaware
Archive Photos, 39
© Archivo Iconografico, S. A./CORBIS, 69
© Bettmann/CORBIS, 18, 62, 67
© CORBIS, 23, 60, 76
Dover Publications, Inc., 25, 50, 58, 74
© Angelo Hornak/CORBIS, 15
Hulton/Archive by Getty Images, 21, 71, 82
The Institute of Texan Cultures, 53
© Michael Nicholson/CORBIS, 28
North Wind Picture Archives, 33, 38, 48, 51
Smithsonian American Art Museum/Art Resource, 14
© Lee Snider/CORBIS, 31, 43

About the Author

Stuart A. Kallen is the author of more than 150 nonfiction books
for children and young adults. He has written on topics ranging
from the theory of relativity to rock-and-roll history to life on the
American frontier. In addition, Mr. Kallen has written award-
winning children's videos and television scripts. In his spare time,
Kallen is a singer/songwriter/guitarist in San Diego, California.